WE TRAILED
THE SIOUX

Pvt. George P. Walker, Company E, 7th Cavalry, left, and Pvt. Timothy Donnelly, Company F, 7th Cavalry, right, struck this devil-may-care pose for an unnamed photographer in 1875. One year later, both men were killed in action near Custer's Hill at the battle of the Little Big Horn. GLEN SWANSON

WE TRAILED THE SIOUX

Enlisted Men Speak on Custer, Crook,
and the Great Sioux War

Paul L. Hedren

STACKPOLE
BOOKS

Published by
STACKPOLE BOOKS
5067 Ritter Road
Mechanicsburg, PA 17055
www.stackpolebooks.com

Printed in the United States of America

10   9   8   7   6   5   4   3   2   1

FIRST EDITION

Library of Congress Cataloging-in-Publication Data

Hedren, Paul L.
  We trailed the Sioux : enlisted men speak on Custer, Crook, and the
Great Sioux War / by Paul Hedren.— 1st ed.
      p. cm.
Includes bibliographical references and index.
ISBN 0-8117-0062-3
  1. Dakota Indians—Wars—Personal narratives. 2. Cheyenne
Indians—Wars—Personal narratives. I.
Title.
E83.876.H425 2003
973.7—dc21

                                                            2002156354

Dedicated to the memory of Don G. Rickey,
who taught us to respect the veterans
of the Indian wars

ALSO BY PAUL L. HEDREN

First Scalp for Custer: The Skirmish at Warbonnet Creek, Nebraska, July 17, 1876 (1980)

With Crook in the Black Hills: Stanley J. Morrow's 1876 Photographic Legacy (1985)

Fort Laramie in 1876, Chronicle of a Frontier Post at War (1988)

Ed., *The Great Sioux War, 1876–77: The Best from* Montana The Magazine of Western History (1991)

Ed., *Campaigning with King: Charles King, Chronicler of the Old Army* (1991)

Travelers Guide to the Great Sioux War: The Battlefields, Forts, and Related Sites of America's Greatest Indian War (1996)

TABLE OF CONTENTS

PREFACE

THIS MONOGRAPH ORIGINATED OUT OF AN INVITATION TO speak at the Third Biennial Fort Robinson History Conference in Nebraska in April 2000. I had been asked to contribute a story about some aspect of enlisted soldier life in the Old Army, that being the theme of the year's conference. I was flattered to be invited and readily agreed to participate, offering on the spot to fashion a story focusing on commoners' views of field service during the Great Sioux War. My vision of the story played directly into two lifelong scholarly interests: the lives and travails of the ordinary soldiers who stocked the Old Army in the years following the Civil War, coupled with an equal passion for the campaigns, battles, broad themes, and minutiae of the prolonged saga now known widely as the Great Sioux War of 1876–77.

Unknown to the conference organizers, I had been toying with this topic for years. It seems as though I grew up cultivating and refining an interest in soldier life in the Trans-Mississippi West, having been an ardent book and frontier militaria collector since childhood, a cavalry reenactor during my college years, a devoted living historian with the National Park

Service early in my working career, and a founding member of the General Miles Marching and Chowder Society, a group still active and easily the nation's finest band of Old Army infantry reenactors. Along the way, I chanced upon several opportunities to research and write on aspects of the frontier army, and I rather diligently collected enlisted accounts of service on the northern plains during the Indian wars era. As for the Fort Robinson History Conference, these consistently sold-out gatherings of historians and enthusiasts of the Old Army occur every other April at this most intriguing western military site featuring, in the view of many devotees, the finest museum in the nation dedicated to the Old Army. The opportunity and venue were perfect.

I titled my presentation "'When We Trailed the Sioux and Heard the War Whoop and Saw the Signal Fires': Enlisted Men Remember the Great Sioux War," chiefly quoting an inscription written by a Sioux War veteran to a brother, figurative or literal, appearing on the front fly of a well-read copy of *Campaigning with Crook*. The book was written by a veteran of the war and indefatigable author, Capt. Charles King, late of the 5th Cavalry. My aim at the onset was to weave an anecdotal story of day-to-day occurrences during the repetitive campaigns against the Sioux and Northern Cheyenne in 1876–77, relying exclusively on diaries, letters, newspaper contributions, and reminiscences penned by enlisted soldiers. Highly literate accounts and diaries written by officers like King, 1st Lt. John G. Bourke, 1st Lt. Edward Godfrey, and 1st Lt. James H. Bradley have always dominated most scholars' attempts at incorporating vivid primary documents into their histories of the war's battles and campaigns. With scattered exceptions, accounts of the conflict penned by the privates, corporals, and sergeants who marched in the ranks were rarely used. I believed that a good story could be fashioned from those writings, and I sought to let the common Regulars tell their story. To be sure, my Fort Robinson presentation and this greatly expanded narrative are an anecdotal tale because, like Indian accounts of the same fighting, these soldiers were not necessarily privy to the campaign and battlefield tactics and strategies that were the domain of their leaders. Instead, these enlisted soldiers crafted personalized expressions of what usually amounted to a narrowly focused daily routine, filled with accounts of hardships, toil, comrades, suffering, and fear, experiences that were, in all, much more ordinary than dramatic or extraordinary. Still, I sought and found exceptions, too.

After plumbing what I think amounts to a truly remarkable collection of enlisted writings, I set out to compose a flowing story of the Great Sioux War using these original voices. Though my intention at the outset was to craft an essay suitable for a thirty-minute presentation, what emerged was a story of far greater length than required for the conference. I carried the story to its end knowing that I could somehow carve the necessary pages from the expanded tale.

With my cause served and my focus duly sharpened, in the months since the Fort Robinson conference, I chased down a handful of other primary wartime accounts and measured those, too, for interesting and different tales of campaigning against the Sioux. What emerged was a fluid narrative

encompassing many aspects of soldiering during an exhaust-
ing yet conclusive twenty-month-long conflict with the
Sioux and Northern Cheyenne. I did not mean to create a
traditional history of the war, since several superb narratives
already exist. Such a history also requires the use of all sources
and not a focused collection such as these enlisted accounts.
And I did not mean to chase every scrap of interview existing
across the nation, particularly in the likes of the renowned
Walter Camp Collections housed in Indiana, Utah, Colorado,
and Montana. Later-day interrogators like Camp communicated with an amazing array of enlisted men, and while I
looked at the modern compilations of those exchanges, I
ended up using a few but not many. Instead, I purposely
sought, catalogued, and incorporated as wide a variety of
meaty accounts of campaigning as I could find. The bibliography from which this story is drawn is itself unique and
includes a welter of truly obscure and unheralded entries
among the well known.

As I crafted this story, I particularly sought out qualities
of service that differentiated veterans' experiences in the
Great Sioux War from the campaigning, combat, and general
field service known in other Indian wars—or, for that matter,
most every other American war. I found two instances that
are uncharacteristic of other warfare in the long narrative of
American military history. I believe them to be defining
moments and dwell on them to some degree.

ACKNOWLEDGMENTS

EVEN SMALL BOOKS REQUIRE HELP FROM FRIENDS, AND I AM grateful to many for contributing accounts or images from personal collections or the repositories in their control, critiquing early drafts of this manuscript, and generally supporting my quest.

I first thank Jim Potter, Brent Carmack, and Larry Sommer, all of Lincoln; Tom Buecker of Fort Robinson; and Eli Paul, now of Overland Park, Kansas, all of whom are, or were, affiliated with the Nebraska State Historical Society and who encouraged my participation in the 2000 Fort Robinson History Conference. This same group has inspired this remarkable history conference since its inception in 1995, and they proudly carry on the tradition with extraordinary élan.

For providing source and photographic materials from their collections or responding to an unusual array of trivial questioning as I searched for this or that name or shadowy detail, I also thank Jerome Greene, Denver, Colorado; Neil Mangum (now of Chiricahua National Monument, Arizona), John Doerner, and Kitty Deer Nose, Little Bighorn Battlefield National Monument, Montana; Paul Fees, Cody, Wyoming; Douglas Scott, Lincoln, Nebraska; B. William Henry, Jr., Grass

Valley, California; Sandy Barnard, Terre Haute, Indiana; Sherry Smith, Dallas, Texas; Greg Martin, Rutherford, California; Jon James, Big Hole National Battlefield, Montana; James Brust, San Pedro, California; Sandra Lowry, Fort Laramie National Historic Site, Wyoming; Lory Morrow, Montana Historical Society; Douglas McChristian, Tucson, Arizona; Peter Cozzens, American Embassy, Panama; Jim Crain, San Francisco, California; Dorothy Neuhaus, Vermillion, South Dakota; William Jones, Nebraska State Historical Society; Larry Ness, Yankton, South Dakota; Susan Reneau, Missoula, Montana; and Glen Swanson, Agua Dulce, California.

Jerry Greene and Peter Cozzens read drafts of the manuscript and provided welcome editorial suggestions. And Leigh Ann Berry and Ryan Masteller of Stackpole Books encouraged and facilitated the project from the outset, also to my great pleasure and betterment of the story.

And finally but most gratefully, I warmly acknowledge Connie Burns of Omaha and my daughters, Ethne and Whitney, of Saint Paul and Northfield, Minnesota, respectively, for reasons they know best; in the case of my inquisitive children, not the least being their willingness to travel with their father to the far-flung places of the Great Sioux War and Dad's pledge to put their names in every book I write.

Paul L. Hedren
O'Neill, Nebraska
November 12, 2002

This dapper, unnamed corporal of Company K, 9th Infantry, spent the Great Sioux War at Camp Robinson, Nebraska. Mixed with routine garrison duties, the corporal frequently patrolled with his company on the Sidney to Black Hills stage and freight road, chased Indians in the nearby Niobrara River valley, and provided martial support during a number of fateful affairs at the adjacent Red Cloud Agency. JEROME A. GREENE

Boots and Saddles

THE ENLISTED MEN FIGHTING IN THE GREAT SIOUX WAR were a curious lot of ordinary Americans thrust unwittingly into one of the West's most compelling dramas. Drawn from every corner of American society, these common soldiers represented its breadth and depth. Among them were youths searching for adventure, immigrants thirsting for an understanding of the nation's ways and language, a cadre of educated men holding well-reasoned views of the circumstances surrounding them, and a scattering of malcontents enduring yet another string of bad days in an already uncertain life. One and all, they slogged the campaign trails of 1876 and 1877, suffering inferior rations, bone-numbing fatigue, scorching summers and freezing winters, and a surprising mortality when they eventually closed with opposing tribesmen. Still, these men went about their business largely out of a simple, loyal call to duty, to comrades, to their regiments, and for the duration of the five-year enlistment each had committed to Uncle Sam's Army.[1]

As one reflects on these soldiers and the enduringly fascinating history of the frontier army, it becomes easy to wish that they had bequeathed subsequent generations a greater written legacy. As a class, these enlisted veterans are not remembered for having penned spellbinding reminiscences of chasing Sitting Bull and Crazy Horse in the nation's centennial year, as did officers like 1st Lt. James H. Bradley, Capt. John G. Bourke, and Capt. Charles King. Few were reporters for hometown newspapers and none stringers for the national media, that being the realm in 1876 and 1877 of Robert E. Strahorn, John F. Finerty, Reuben B. Davenport, Charles S. Diehl, and others writing for metropolitan newspapers in New York City, Chicago, San Francisco, and elsewhere. And no enlisted man's wife penned a glowing memorial to her husband's service in the 1870s as did officers' wives like Cynthia Capron, Elizabeth Burt, and Elizabeth B. Custer. But should we conclude, therefore, that the enlisted men engaged in the Great Sioux War had no voices whatsoever? Quite to the contrary, a surprising number were diligent daily diarists who recorded life on the campaign trail in the company of fellow soldiers, a few did occasionally write to local newspapers, and a fair number found time months and years later to pen reminiscences of this alluring epic. And because of the almost immediate fascination with Custer and the enigmatic Little Big Horn battle, dogged interrogators like Walter Camp and Thomas Marquis particularly sought out 7th Cavalry veterans and reaped from them wonderful accounts of that engagement and its prelude and aftermath.

Remarkably, an enlisted voice exists for nearly every significant movement of this twenty-month-long northern plains Indian war, whether the participant patrolled a Black

Hills stage road, garrisoned a Yellowstone River supply depot, guarded a steamboat, or marched with a well-known commander. And while enlisted men richly detailed larger movements such as Brig. Gen. Alfred Terry's Dakota column and Brig. Gen. George Crook's Big Horn and Yellowstone Expedition, and actions like Little Big Horn and Slim Buttes, so too did they describe less dramatic episodes like the Warbonnet Creek action and the 1877 Little Missouri Expedition.[2]

The vibrancy of the soldiers' recountings is surprising as well. Their diaries are replete with such unadorned observations as "marched twelve miles, no wood, bad water," and "Rainy all day. Went fishing but did not get a bite, only from the mosquitos." But so, too, are they filled with commentary on the humility of eating horseflesh, the utter deprivation of the cold, wet, and muddy "Starvation March," and even the general worthiness of their commanders. And while the 7th Cavalry's later-day interrogators were understandably riveted on Custer's, Reno's, Benteen's, and Weir's movements at the Little Big Horn, frequently did the veterans amplify their tales with such memories as John Tanner's death on Reno Hill, Mike Madden's amputation, or burning numbers on tepee poles with heated ramrods to mark officers' graves on Custer Hill. Dissected and given context, this enlisted men's legacy is remarkably informative, often spellbinding, and in many instances delightfully original.

──── ══◆══ ────

The successive campaigns against the Lakota and Northern Cheyenne Indians engulfing American Regular army troops in the mid-1870s began simply enough. Lieutenant General Philip H. Sheridan, commander of the Military Division of the Missouri, and his Dakota and Platte department commanders, Terry and Crook, envisioned three converging columns penetrating the Powder and Yellowstone River country of Wyoming and Montana. There they would engage scattered Sioux bands and force their return to the Great Sioux Reservation and its agencies in Nebraska and along the Missouri River. These Indians had never embraced the agencies or any sense of government control and posed perceived and real threats to the emigrant miners steadily invading the Black Hills in southwestern Dakota Territory. The Black Hills lay almost squarely within the bounds of the Sioux reservation, and their opening was a political imbroglio engulfing the administration of President Ulysses S. Grant. An attempt to purchase the Hills failed in 1875, and Grant finally acquiesced to a military campaign to stem Indian resistance across the northern plains. The generals envisioned a short war.[3]

Crook was the first to respond, marching north from Fort Fetterman, Wyoming, in March 1876. A devastating clash with Northern Cheyenne on the Powder River thwarted his advance and prompted an ignoble return to Fetterman to reorganize. The engagement also brought the Northern Cheyenne people, long friendly with the Sioux, into the conflict.[4]

The classic summer movement against these northern roamers, as the nonagency people came to be known, the details of which are recited so easily by aficionados of Custer's Little Big Horn campaign, commenced in May 1876.

Columns commanded by Crook, marching again from the south; Terry, marching westward from the Missouri River in Dakota Territory; and Col. John Gibbon, coursing eastward from western Montana, struck the field, aimed one and all at the same untamed Indian country. In June the Sioux battered Crook on Rosebud Creek and repulsed and destroyed Custer on the Little Big Horn River, both in southeastern Montana, in battles of such enormity as to readily obscure the regrouping and persistent prolonged campaigning that ensued. Of Custer's fight, combatants and distant observers alike had much to say. Only in hindsight did the world comprehend how the Indians' extraordinary ascendance in June 1876 that produced those glorious victories ended the moment the tribesmen departed the Little Big Horn valley. The powerful Indian coalition never again recomposed, and the generals resolved for victory at all costs.[5]

But first the summer campaign sputtered. Sheridan had already begun deploying additional troops to other sectors of the vast war zone fronting the Indian agencies, the southern margins of the Black Hills gold fields, and the wild Upper Missouri country. In mid-June 1876, for instance, elements of the 5th Cavalry regiment were dispatched from the Department of the Missouri to safeguard the treacherous Black Hills road north of Fort Laramie. In mid-July the 5th clashed with a Cheyenne band headed for the victorious northern camps. At Warbonnet Creek, Nebraska, the 5th's chief of scouts, William F. Cody, lofted the "first scalp for Custer." In due course, the regiment was redirected to Crook's Big Horn and Yellowstone Expedition, and their stead on the southern periphery of the

Black Hills was taken by the 4th Cavalry regiment, also trans-
ferred from the Department of the Missouri.[6]

At the same time, elements of the 5th, 11th, and 22nd
Infantry and 4th Artillery were drawn from across the nation
for service in the war zone, and particularly in Terry's beleaguered Department of Dakota. Of them, infantry commanded by Col. Nelson A. Miles and Lt. Col. Elwell S. Otis
soon hutted themselves at the confluence of the Tongue and
Yellowstone rivers and commenced relentless independent
campaigning in the fall and winter against Sitting Bull's and
Crazy Horse's bands. Decisive engagements at Cedar and Ash
creeks north of the Yellowstone, and on the Tongue River
south of the Yellowstone, among many smaller demonstrations
of purpose, broke the warriors' resolve and contributed
directly to surrenders at the agencies or, for some, flight to
Canada.[7]

As the summer of 1876 waned, Crook ambled from the
Yellowstone River eastward, determined to press the fighting
in the Dakota badlands and toward the Black Hills and his
own Platte Department in Nebraska and Wyoming. Although
he was desperately short of provisions, Crook's trail soon
turned southward, following shadowy Indian signs. In the
midst of an inglorious and agonizing period in which his soldiers survived by eating their own worn pack mules and cavalry horses, an advance guard chanced upon a Sioux camp in
the Slim Buttes north of the Black Hills. The village was
routed, and winter provisions discovered in the tepees sus-
tained the soldiers a short while longer as they plodded
southward again to the gold camps. The hardships endured on

this march gave Crook's solders much to write about, and their anguish and bitterness are palpable.[8]

Crook reorganized for yet a third time in the fall and led the 4th Cavalry and other fresh troops northward from Fort Fetterman in mid-November 1876. On November 25, a cavalry command led by Col. Ranald Mackenzie struck a Northern Cheyenne village in the southern Big Horn Mountains and inflicted a devastating blow that soon ended that tribe's participation in the Great Sioux War. Crook disbanded his expedition as winter settled permanently across the northern plains but anticipated taking the field again when mild weather returned.[9]

For the Boys of '76, Miles's and Crook's persistent campaigning in Wyoming and Montana brought evident results in the spring of 1877. Massive surrenders, including Crazy Horse's at Camp Robinson on May 6, proved to the generals that the great war had been won. And yet a few scattered tribesmen held out in Montana, and Sitting Bull and others sought refuge in Canada. Unwilling to prematurely close the active campaigning before success was absolutely assured, Crook dispatched elements of the 5th Cavalry into northern Wyoming to deter any notions at the agencies of bands returning to the hunting lands. Miles, meanwhile, clashed on May 7, 1877, with a large, resistant band on Muddy Creek, south of the Yellowstone. As well, he organized sizable columns of troops directed to scour southeastern Montana and western Dakota and, like the 5th Cavalry in Wyoming, demonstrate to the Sioux the futility of abandoning the agencies.[10]

On twenty-two different fields in Nebraska, Wyoming, Montana, North Dakota, and South Dakota, blood was shed during the long course of the Great Sioux War.[11] American history had seen nothing like it before, and its legacy would not be repeated. Before its end, nearly one-quarter of the American Regular army was engaged on the northern plains, and what the common men of that extraordinary endeavor thought, felt, and endured warrants remembering.

Sergeant Daniel A. Kanipe, Company C, 7th Cavalry, rode with Custer at the Little Big Horn, but as the battle unfolded, he opportunely carried a verbal message from Custer to Capt. Thomas M. McDougall to hurry along the ammunition-laden pack train. Kanipe subsequently fought bravely in Major Reno's hilltop fight while his company fell with Custer. LITTLE BIGHORN BATTLEFIELD NATIONAL MONUMENT

2

Charge

SHERIDAN, TERRY, CROOK, AND MOST COMMISSIONED OFFI-cers easily explained why American Regulars waged war against the Sioux and their allies in 1876 and 1877, pointing at what they believed to be the arrogance of the northern roamers, the economic boon of the Black Hills gold fields, and the national desirability of completing a northern transcontinental railroad. In their various writings, however, the enlisted men engaged in the conflict were mostly silent regarding the roots of the war and the prospects for, and haz-ards of, field service. But when a soldier did express himself on the matter, his view went straight to the point. "Its all in account of their being forced out of their rations and the miners going in the Hills and their possessions," wrote the 7th Cavalry's Pvt. Marion Horn to his sister before Custer's cam-paign began. The officers were right and so was Horn, a casu-alty at the Little Big Horn.[12]

All soldiers comprehended the dangers of Indian fighting, but field service was often bizarrely welcomed as a counter to the monotony of garrison life. Perhaps William White, a 2nd Cavalry private marching with Gibbon, captured the enlisted men's attitude on this point. "Everybody was speculating on what would be the plan and the procedure," he wrote. But "nobody was in the least doubt as to what would be the outcome. It simply was this: We United States soldiers were going to wipe up the earth with those impudent Indians."[13] That field service might result in death, however, nagged some men. Seventh Cavalryman John Ryan, the first sergeant of Company M, wrote of his friend James Turley's request at Fort Rice to care for his personal property if he died in the coming campaign. Both agreed that if either was killed, the survivor would gain the other's possessions. Private Turley perished in Reno's valley fight at the Little Big Horn when his horse bolted into the Indian camp. "He was a very nice young man," remembered Ryan.[14] Sergeant John Powers of the 5th Cavalry, marching north of Fort Laramie with Eugene Carr, wrote more plaintively of the start of the campaigning but expressed what most of the men must have felt: "The boys are all in good spirits, and eager to be in active service."[15]

For all the unfolding drama of the Great Sioux War, the initial movements to the front were generally monotonous and dreary. Each of the columns followed well-established roads, whether west from Fort Abraham Lincoln, Dakota; north from Fort Fetterman, Wyoming; or east from Fort Ellis, Montana. Once seasoned to the routine of daily marches and unassuming camps, the diarists tell us little more about their first days in the field aside from road conditions, weather, the availability of firewood, and the potability of the water. Different segments of the respective columns found ways to accommodate one another, of course. The sizable mule trains in

Crook's Big Horn and Yellowstone Expedition, for instance, typically moved in single file alongside the column of troops, about fifty yards off the trail. "We were always on the lee side," remembered packer Henry Daly, "so the troops didn't get our dust, but we got theirs."[16] And there was no parade ground formality to the marches. As the companies and battalions fell in day to day, "Route step, march" was the typical call commencing a paced but uncadenced advance. Major Alexander Chambers, commander of Crook's infantry battalion, was so predictable in his informal marching routine that he quickly gained the nickname "Route Step Chambers," since he always barked that command immediately after the order to march. "He was one of the most methodical officers I ever served under," remembered 14th Infantryman William Jordan.[17]

In their writings, the soldiers understandably paid particular attention to the availability of wood and water and the sufficiency of their rations, and at the start no conditions were worse than undrinkable water and a cold camp. When the columns traversed the treeless prairies of Dakota and Wyoming, firewood was scarce. But the men quickly learned to use bunched grass, sagebrush, and buffalo chips to fry their pork and brew their coffee. Rain dampened those prospects frequently, however, and so did snow. During Crook's Powder River Expedition in November and December 1876, Sgt. James Kincaid of the 4th Cavalry recalled one particularly woodless camp where the men resorted to digging buffalo chips from beneath the snow. "Imagine the 1,200 wet, hungry, and half frozen men scattered over the prairie, when the ground was covered with snow ten inches deep, hunting buffalo chips."[18] William Zimmer, an intuitive twenty-nine-year-old private of the 2nd Cavalry, remembered a woodless camp the following summer in western Dakota. "We have no wood this evening, so we are again euchred out of a warm supper."[19] And even if firewood could be found, there were occasions on the campaign trail when fires were not permitted out of fear that smoke would betray the soldiers' presence in Indian country. Remembered packer David Mears of an occasion during Crook's Powder River campaign: "We dared not build a fire. . . . Our spread for dinner was frozen beans, frozen bread, with snow balls and pepper on the side; supper the same, less the beans. We began to think that the government was treating us rather cool."[20]

Bad water tormented the troops, too. Twenty-one-year-old Pvt. James Frew of the 5th Cavalry remembered the regiment's Cheyenne River camp north of Fort Laramie in June 1876 as a place with "very bad water. Water thick as cream with alkali."[21] The water in Montana's Pumpkin Creek was equally poor that summer. "Water in this stream about the color of yellow ochre, and as thick as mud," quipped 14th Infantryman Jordan. "In fact," he added, "we could not make coffee with it, or at least when made it had not the slightest taste of coffee."[22]

Typically, salt pork, coffee, hard crackers, and sugar constituted the standard ration for Regular troops on campaign. Corporal John Zimmerman of the 14th Infantry, marching with Crook, described the allowances in particular detail. "Each man was issued his days rations separately every night as follows, three tablespoonsful of ground coffee, three tablespoonsful sugar, three of beans or rice, twelve crackers (four inches square), [and] twelve ounces of bacon."[23] The various commands managed rations differently, depending on circumstances and the availability of a continuing supply. By midsummer 1876, Crook's men received rations every two days, which they ate "in one day," remembered Frew.[24] Private Wilmont Sanford of the 6th Infantry, on depot guard at the mouth of the Powder River, remembered drawing a bacon ration every night, and coffee and sugar once every fourth day. Sanford's beans came green, however, and roasting coffee became just another of the regular camp chores.[25] When camps were prolonged, as on Goose Creek, Wyoming, and the Yellowstone, the daily fare was occasionally augmented. In season, soldiers discovered lamb's-quarter and wild onions, for instance, which they quickly added to their diets. Flour and navy beans were occasionally issued, too, which creative cooks sometimes transformed, respectively, into donuts and bean soup.[26]

When circumstances allowed, the campaigners proved to be energetic hunters and fishermen. Buffalo, deer, elk, pronghorn, rabbits, prairie dogs, prairie chickens, geese, and ducks were delivered to the camps with frequency, but more often to supplement officers' messes and not always those of the enlisted men. There were exceptions, of course. On July 10, 1876, Sgt. George Howard of the 2nd Cavalry remembered some sixty killed elk being delivered to Crook's camp and how most everyone enjoyed fresh elk steaks that evening.[27] Scouts regularly delivered fresh game to the camps. Trumpeter Henry Dose of Company G, 7th Cavalry, wrote to his wife of getting antelope meat from "them Indian scouts, but had to pay $2.00 for a quarter of it."[28] Scouts delivered buffalo meat that was typically fashioned into stew by the 6th Infantry companies guarding the Yellowstone. One evening in November, one of Col. Ranald Mackenzie's Indian scouts delivered an antelope to that officer's mess, and he shared it with his orderlies. "That made us a good meal," remembered Pvt. William Smith of the 4th Cavalry. "We had more to eat than if we had been in our company."[29] A year later, again on the Yellowstone during the futile campaigning that season, 7th Cavalryman Ami Mulford remembered his squad chancing upon a small herd of buffalo. They gave chase and killed one. "We had 'Indian beef' for supper," Mulford boasted.[30]

Perhaps no camp diversion was as rewarding as fishing, which the enlisted men enjoyed with a distinct relish. Crook's prolonged summer camp along Goose Creek, Wyoming, offered unprecedented opportunities for angling in fresh mountain-fed waters, and the men lined the streams nearly every day. Sergeant Howard recorded his company's haul of ninety-three mountain trout one day, each weighing from one-half to three pounds. His personal catch another day was ten trout, weighing together seventeen and three-quarter pounds. "This is the grandest, finest sport I ever saw!" he reported.[31] For the enlisted men traveling across the Big Horn Mountains with Sheridan in July 1877 en route to inspect the Custer battlefield, sport fishing meant discharging their weapons into small mountain pools and collecting per-cussion-stunned trout when they floated to the surface.[32] On the Yellowstone River, even the steamboat guards fished, "every time the boat stops," remembered 6th Infantryman Sanford. Fishing was evidently always productive on the Yellowstone, whether for trout on the upper reaches or catfish on the lower half. In 1877, Private Zimmer of the 2nd Cavalry wrote of the "splendid cat fishing here. The boys catch lots, and large ones."[33] Despite these occasional successes at augmenting the standard army field ration, hunting and fishing triumphs were sporadic at best. Private Ami Mulford summed it up with this quip: "We now have a change of diet; hard-tack, bacon and coffee for breakfast; raw bacon and tack for dinner; fried bacon and hard bread for supper."[34]

⸻

Long daily marches, relatively cheerless evening camps, and occasional successes at foraging and fishing became day-to-day repetitions as well-armed and reasonably seasoned soldiers were ushered to the front, with the prospect of closing with the Sioux and Cheyenne. Alone among the field officers at the start of the 1876 campaign, George Custer of the 7th Cavalry fixated on the chance of scoring a telling victory over the tribesmen. Custer's obsession was not held by other commanders or the men in the ranks, but all who participated in the Little Big Horn affair of June 25 through 28, whether a survivor or rescuer, remembered the occasion for the rest of their lives. Little Big Horn's monumental dimension, in fact, quickly became a defining episode of both the Great Sioux War and the long history of the settlement of the American West.

In and of itself, the 7th's push to the Little Big Horn sparkled with manly fortitude as the men endured repetitive hard marches, precious little sleep, and cold rations. On the morning of the battle, First Sergeant Ryan of Company M, a vigorous, seasoned veteran of the Civil War and other earlier 7th Cavalry campaigns, recalled a brief pause on the trail and how the men simply dropped to the ground without unsaddling their horses, threw reins over their arms, and went to sleep.[35] At this halt, some made coffee. "I remember this very distinctly," wrote Pvt. William Slaper of Ryan's company, "because I did not get any of the coffee, having dropped down under a tree and fallen asleep . . . and I did not awaken until called to fall into line."[36] "Those who did not care to sleep sat around in little groups discussing the prospects of a fight and pulling at the ever present pipe," recalled William Taylor, a thirty-one-year-old private of Company A.[37] Later, before crossing the divide into the Little Big Horn valley, most men ate a soldier breakfast and, remembered Ryan, "for our bill of fare had raw bacon, hardtack, and cold water, which we relished very much."[38]

After a little rest and a bite to eat, the men of Custer's regiment became talkative, and speculation ran high on how soon the campaign would end. Remembered Pvt. Peter Thompson of Company E:

> One old soldier said that it would end just as soon as we could reach old Sitting Bull. Another said, "If that is all, the campaign will soon be over, and Custer will take us with him to the Centennial." "Of course," said a wag, "we will take Sitting Bull with us." This created a roar of laughter among those who heard

him. The conversation continued, each one telling his
neighbor what he would take when Sitting Bull's
camp was captured. This was on the morning of the
25th of June, 1876, a day I will never forget as long as
I live.[39]

Later, as the great battle opened, 2nd Lt. Charles A. Varnum was seen swinging his hat in the air and shouting to his
men, "'Thirty days furlough to the man who gets the first
scalp.' We were very anxious for the furlough, but not so particular about the scalp," recalled Ryan.[40]

To be under fire for the first time in one's life certainly
quickens the pulse and fixes the moment. Private Slaper was
perfectly clear about this. Among the troops opening the battle with Reno in the Little Big Horn valley, the Company M
trooper remembered: "Soon commenced the rattle of rifle
fire, and bullets began to whistle about us. I remember that I
ducked my head and tried to dodge bullets which I could
hear whizzing through the air. This was my first experience
under fire. I know that for a time I was frightened, and far
more so when I got my first glimpse of the Indians riding
about in all directions, firing at us and yelling and whooping
like incarnate fiends."[41] Slaper's first sergeant, John Ryan, also
clearly remembered that moment. "Before we arrived at the
timber, there was one shot fired away ahead of us. I did not
know whether it was fired by Lieutenant Varnum's scouts or
one of the hostile Indians. That was the first shot that I heard
in the opening of the battle of the Little Big Horn on June
25, 1876, and I had pretty good ears about that time."[42]

Another diarist, Private Smith of the 4th Cavalry, penned the same sentiment about the November battle on the Red Fork of the Powder River. Of that, he wrote, "Bullets were flying every way and mighty close too. I had my pistol in my hand and felt a little rattled, I must say, for this was the first time I had ever heard them so close."[43]

The valley fight at the Little Big Horn was chaotic and utterly mismanaged, and it soon progressed away from the village and onto the bluffs across and upriver from Reno's opening position. There the major's men entrenched and endured a lively siege that lasted through the evening of June 26. The men did their best to dig in but were hampered by the lack of spades. Recalled Private Slaper: "I used my butcher knife to cut the earth loose and throw a mound of it in front of me upon which to rest my carbine. At one time a bullet struck the corner of this mound, throwing so much dirt into my eyes that I could scarcely see for an hour or more."[44] First Sergeant Ryan also remembered the pitiful tools at hand, which consisted of "two spades, our knives and tin cups, and, in fact, we used pieces of hard tack boxes for spades. . . . We also formed breastworks from boxes of hard bread, sacks of bacon, sacks of corn and oats, blankets, and in fact everything that we could get hold of."[45]

The siege on the bluff top tried the men in many ways. Despite attempts at making breastworks, some positions were continually exposed to both frontal and enfilading fire. Bullets scattered dirt, tore off boot heels, struck the horses, and killed men. In one instance, in scattering attackers who had crept close to the southern line, Pvt. James Tanner of Company M was badly wounded and unable to return to the breastworks. First Sergeant Ryan and three others rushed to his assistance, "rolled him into a blanket, and made quick tracks in getting him from the side of the bluffs to where [their] wounded lay. Fortunately none of the rescuing party received anything more than a few balls through their clothing. After placing Tanner with the rest of the wounded, he died in a few minutes."[46]

Frank Mann, a civilian packer, was as unlucky as Tanner. Mann had been engaged in long-range shooting with a standard-issue Springfield cavalry carbine. Remembered Corp. Stanislas Roy of Company A: "He was . . . on A Company's line. He was aiming . . . over a breastwork about three feet high, and after he had been observed in this position about twenty minutes, someone [remarked] that 'something must be wrong with the packer.' Upon going up he was found stone dead, having been hit in the temple and killed so quick that he did not move from [the] position [of] sighting his gun."[47] Elsewhere on the line, the soldier lying next to Private Thompson of Company E was equally luckless. Remembered Thompson, he was "sheltered by a cracker box and talking in a cheerful manner about the possibilities of us getting out of our present difficulty, when a ball came crashing through the box hitting him and killing him instantly. There was but one gasp and all was still."[48]

As the engagement wore on, the men with Reno and Capt. Frederick Benteen suffered mightily from thirst, hunger, and the lack of sleep. Private Thomas O'Neill of Company G remembered being so thirsty that his mouth would make no saliva, and when he tried eating a hard cracker, he could not swallow at all, but blew the food out of his mouth as dry as so much flour.[49] Corporal Roy of Company A chewed grass to get saliva up.[50] Private Taylor, also of Company A, wrote of chewing lead from a bullet, gnawing on the inner part of the prickly pear cactus, and holding pebbles in the mouth, but "all were useless, if not an aggravation."[51]

Thirsts became so acute, especially among the wounded, that at midday on June 26, a few volunteers descended the bluffs under devastating Indian fire, filled camp kettles and canteens with river water, and regained the defensive works. The initial water run took nearly ninety minutes and was repeated several times. "Dr. Porter issued water to the wounded, but there was not enough to give them all they craved for," recalled Roy.[52] Only after the warriors and villagers withdrew under cover of darkness on the twenty-sixth were the soldiers finally able to secure adequate water for the men and horses. "They left us masters of the field, but how dearly bought, forty-two wounded, fourteen killed," Pvt. Thomas Coleman wrote cryptically but so reflectively in his diary as he lay in the trenches that night.[53]

One of the more colorful casualties of the heroic water quest was Pvt. Mike Madden of Company K, a burly forty-year-old Irish saddler whose lower right leg had been shattered by a bullet. His company commander, 1st Lt. Edward Godfrey, had him retrieved later in the day and delivered to Dr. Henry Porter's makeshift hospital in the midst of the entrenchment area. After the battle, Madden was removed to Gibbon's camp in the valley, where Porter amputated the saddler's leg just below the knee, and in doing so gave rise to one of the most popular contemporary anecdotes emanating from the Great Sioux War. Before commencing the amputation, Porter gave Madden a stiff horn of brandy to brace him up. The saddler went through the ordeal with nary a whimper and was given another drink, whereupon he was supposedly overheard saying to the surgeon that if he'd allow him yet one more swig, he could "cut off me other leg!" The story became an oft-repeated regimental parable so long as Little Big Horn veterans survived, and despite Madden's display of humor, his battle experiences resonate with extraordinary courage.[54]

Barely eight miles north of the Reno–Benteen entrenchments, the combined Terry and Gibbon command encamped on the evening of June 26 after a difficult and ominous march up the Little Big Horn valley. Earlier that day, they had received indications of a great battle and defeat, but no one could yet appreciate the calamity that had already unfolded. That day, Gibbon's cavalry had exchanged shots with elusive warriors, and their presence and evident determination had threatening overtones. Musician George Berry of Company E, 7th Infantry, recalled the occasion clearly. "It was late in the evening and we did not know what was ahead of us, so we camped just before dark. The Infantry camped in form of a hollow square, and nobody took any clothes off. Each man slept with his rifle beside him, and each one had a belt full of cartridges. This was on the 26th of June and I had served just four years, leaving me one year of a five year enlistment and of course, I remembered this date."[55] The talk in the camp was haunting. At sunset some of Gibbon's scouts had observed "strange-looking objects" on the long ridge across the valley east of them. The scouts decided they were dead buffalo. "A topic for conversation was not lacking that night," recalled 7th Infantryman William White. "Theories were advanced," he said. "Other theories met them. Arguments ensued. The average hours of sleep per man were greatly diminished. [But] nobody . . . supposed [Custer] was dead."[56]

Terry's and Gibbon's cavalry and infantry marched cautiously southward on the morning of June 27. Private Homer Coon of Company G, 7th Infantry, remembered the deliberate pace as the soldiers approached the Indian village:

> We entered their deserted camp, seeing no signs of life. First Lieutenant Bradley of the Seventh Infantry was scouting the other side of the Little Big Horn River with ten mounted men. We saw them dismount as for a rest, our command was resting at the time. We had started on the hike again when we saw a horseman coming down the slope towards us waving his big hat. We talked, he swam the river, came through the strip of timber, and headed for the head of the column, handing a dispatch to General Terry. It was young Rice of H company coming down the line saying Custer was wiped out, saying they were all dead, as Lieutenant Bradley thought the Sioux had got the whole regiment. We took up the hike through the deserted camp and as we got further in we saw dead bodies lying on the ground, some with

arrows sticking in them, which some of the boys pulled out. They were horribly mutilated. We were all positive now that there were no survivors, but as we got further in we saw moving objects across the river on a high knoll about two miles distant.[57]

As dawn broke, meanwhile, in the Reno–Benteen entrenchments on June 27, Pvt. Theodore W. Goldin of Company G, 7th Cavalry, reflected on his regiment's travails:

The first rays of the morning sun . . . shone down into the Little Big Horn Valley and wakened into life the disheartened remnant of the once gallant Seventh, who for thirty-six hours, without rest, food, or drink, had been stubbornly contesting for their lives against the overwhelming force of Indians hurled against them, but now worn out and discouraged . . . they were grouped together around their rifle pits, speculating on the sudden departure of the enemy late the preceding afternoon.[58]

A trumpeter's shrill notes of "Recall" echoing across the valley sent the survivors into a state of wild excitement. Wrote Goldin:

Everyone was watching a cloud of dust far down the river which seemed to be moving rapidly in our direction. A few moments later and the blue flag, with the single white star in the center, which we knew to designate the headquarters of General Terry, could be seen in the advance. Like lightning the news flashed down the line, "Terry is here!" Cheer after cheer rose from the entrenchments, feebly echoed from the poor wounded fellows in the hospital.[59]

Remembered Daniel Kanipe, a twenty-three-year-old sergeant in Company C: "General Terry and staff came up to us on the bluff and informed us of the massacre of General Custer and his five troops. We had supposed that he and his men were corralled at some other point, as we were at this one. When General Terry came up, the boys gave him three cheers. He cried like a child as he told us of Custer's sad fate."[60] Terry particularly sought out the wounded men in the hospital. He moved among the sufferers, recalled Goldin, "speaking words of cheer and dispensing hearty hand clasps. Not a man was missed; he had a kind word and a sympathetic grip for all. As the full extent of our loss became more and more evident, and as the poor, wounded fellows, cheered by his presence, feebly tried to smile their thanks for his visit, tears coursed unheeded and unchecked down his bronzed and bearded cheeks."[61]

The combined infantry and cavalry forces spent the next two days gingerly moving Reno's wounded from the bluffs to the valley, exploring the hastily abandoned yet remarkably fascinating Indian village, and burying dead comrades. No one could be prepared for the carnage strewn across the ridges east of the river where Custer's men fought and died. The principal work of burying the casualties consumed nearly all of the twenty-eighth, and for most, the so-called burials amounted to little more than respectful gestures. The survivors had few spades and mostly used knives, bayonets, and cups to scrape shallow depressions for the bodies. Recalled White: "In some cases the scooping out of the surface ground was omitted, the body being simply straightened out—or maybe not even straightened out—and covered with sagebrush and a little dirt and sand. The state of putridity consequent upon the two or more days of exposure during the long and hot daylight hours rendered any handling almost impractical."[62]

The mutilations inflicted on the dead and the presence of badly wounded but still living cavalry horses further intensified emotions and instilled visions of grisly combat that haunted these veterans for the remainder of their lives. Near where Custer was found, Pvt. George Glenn of Company H, 7th Cavalry, discovered the body of former bunky Tom Tweed of Company L. "His crotch had been split up with an ax and one of his legs thrown up over his shoulder. He was shot with arrows in both eyes. A wounded horse lay near him groaning, and we knocked him in the head with a bloody ax that lay near by, evidently one that had been used by the Indians to cut up or mutilate the wounded."[63] "Some of these disfigurations were too horrible to mention," recalled Private Slaper. "After being scalped, the skulls were crushed in with stone hammers, and the bodies cut and slashed in all the fleshy portions."[64] As the burial parties went about their emotion-wrenching chore, "the eyes of surviving comrades were filled with tears, and throats were choked with grief unspeakable," remembered interpreter Frederic F. Gerard.[65]

While the 7th Cavalry's enlisted casualties received only the scantiest of burials, most of the officers were more carefully interred. "I was working a spade," remembered Slaper, and "I am sure that we used more earth in covering Custer's body, and made a larger mound for it than for any of the others." To more particularly mark these graves, Sgt. George Gaffney of Company I, 7th Cavalry, was ordered by the 7th's quartermaster, 1st Lt. Henry J. Nowland, to cut up tepee poles from the village and drive them into the ground where officers' bodies were buried. "Each was marked with a Roman numeral burned on with a heated ramrod," remembered Gaffney.[66]

In these hours immediately after the battle, the survivors faced other poignant moments. Stanislas Roy remembered leading horses from the entrenchments to the river. "It was a pitiful sight to see the poor animals plunge their heads in the water up to their eyes and drink," he recalled. On June 28 Roy was detailed to shoot some twenty wounded horses scattered on the bluffs and abandoned during the battle, along with some that had been turned loose after being wounded.[67] Private Francis Kennedy, a lucky survivor of the decimated Company I commanded by Keogh, having been detached to the pack train, recalled discovering Keogh's horse Comanche standing, but horribly wounded, in the northern end of the village:

> He was not able to move . . . and had, I should guess, about twenty wounds, some flesh wounds and some more serious. I went hunting around and finally

found a camp kettle and went down to the river to get some water, taking some into my hands and washing out his wounds as best I could. We got him down to the river and after getting him there, we met a corporal of the Seventh Cavalry and he was detailed to shoot all of the wounded animals. Corporal Reynolds was his name. I asked him to let Comanche stand still until I could get an order from Reno not to have [him] shot. I got this order.[68]

When the horrifying burial work on the hillsides was largely finished, many of the men sought moments to explore the Indian village, which proved both an inviting curiosity and an extension of the battlefield's dread. Remembered Musician Berry of Gibbon's 7th Infantry: "It surely looked as though they left in a hurry, and lots of their camp equipage was left behind. I saw lodge poles, buffalo robes, pots and pans galore and in one place I saw a stack of new milk pans which no doubt had been taken from some settler." Seventh Cavalryman Peter Thompson remembered seeing "quite a number of stone mallets covered with hair and blood, which had undoubtedly been used by the squaws on the heads of the dead and wounded soldiers."[69]

Where Reno had crossed the Little Big Horn in retreat, George Herendeen, one of Gibbon's civilian scouts, recalled finding a dead horse. "This horse lay in water too shallow to float him off," he told Walter Camp. "Upon investigation we found a dead soldier under him. Whether he had been drowned by being caught under the horse when the latter fell, or whether he had been killed simultaneously with the horse I do not know."[70] The men discovered the remains of other 7th Cavalry casualties in the village, including Pvt. John Armstrong of Company A, who, Sgt. John Hammon remembered, was "beheaded and his head stuck on a pole";[71] Isaiah Dorman, the Negro scout and interpreter, whom Private Slaper remembered seeing "with many arrows shot into his body and head, and badly cut and slashed"; and Jim Turley, John Ryan's friend, whose "body was found with his hunting knife driven to the hilt in one eye."[72] After hastily destroying the lodge poles and cooking utensils littering the abandoned camp, the men gladly departed the village, wherein, too, the stench had become unbearable.[73]

But the ordeal for the 7th Cavalry's wounded was not yet finished. The steamboat *Far West* awaited at the mouth of the Little Big Horn, seventeen miles north, to evacuate these men to medical care at Fort Abraham Lincoln. But gaining the boat without further harming the afflicted was as much an ordeal for the bearers as the transported. Initially the wounded were ushered north in litters borne by infantrymen. "Two men were supposed to carry one wounded man," remembered Musician Berry. "My partner said he weighed 125 pounds and I didn't weigh much more at the time." Berry's wounded soldier weighed 185 pounds, and "he was badly wounded, too . . . shot in the small of the back, and didn't want to be put on the ground any oftener than could be avoided; but we had to set him down pretty often in order to rest, as there was no road, and after dark we kept tripping over weeds and sage brush."[74] Poor Mike Madden, the amputee, was dropped to the ground twice, "but he never uttered a complaint," Pvt. Thomas Coleman of Company B, 7th Cavalry, scrawled in his diary.[75] Eventually fit cavalrymen became bearers, too, with four men assigned to the individual litters. Of the humanitarian ordeal, 7th Infantry Pvt. Edward Stumpf recalled, "It was one of the most trying jobs I ever experienced, dark, no road, hill up, hill down, the wounded moaning, groaning and us tired to death."[76]

Private Taylor of the 7th Cavalry remembered arriving at the *Far West:*

> About one o'clock in the morning the head of the column, looming weirdly through the darkness in the flickering firelight, approached the boat. Captain Marsh had caused a portion of the deck to be thickly covered with grass, and over it had spread a lot of tent flies, making the whole like an immense mattress and in a short time, the fifty-two stricken men were placed on board and with them Keogh's horse, Comanche. The men were laid in rows on the grass covered deck and Drs. Williams and H. R. Porter set about examining and dressing their wounds.[77]

Interestingly, one of the wounded troopers, Sgt. Henry Weihe of Company M, felt snubbed by the officers of his own regiment. As the men were being made comfortable on the boat, he wrote, "The officers of the other regiment were very kind to us, but our own officers kept their distance, with the exception of Col. Weir—he was very kind and considerate toward the wounded, and they all remembered him for it."[78]

Private Frederick G. Bond, Company G, 17th Infantry, spent much
of the summer of 1876 guarding the Rosebud Creek and Powder
River supply camps on the Yellowstone River. In mid–October he
was among the companies engaged by Sitting Bull's warriors at
Spring Creek, Montana, in a running fight occurring between the
Glendive supply depot and Col. Nelson Miles's new Tongue River
Cantonment. Bond is wearing the unpopular but functional floppy-
brimmed 1872 black campaign hat and the army's standard-issue
gray wool shirt. GENERAL RESEARCH DIVISION, NEW YORK PUBLIC LIBRARY,
ASTOR, LENOX AND TILDEN FOUNDATIONS

3

The General

IN THE WAKE OF THE DEVASTATING BATTLE OF THE LITTLE BIG
Horn, the campaign against the Sioux ground to a halt. Terry
and Gibbon retired to a semipermanent camp on the Yellowstone east of the Big Horn confluence, and Crook remained
encamped along Goose Creek, at the eastern foot of the Big
Horn Mountains in Wyoming. Both commands sought reinforcements, feinted advances against the intimidating and
seemingly invincible tribesmen, and generally languished in a
demoralized state. At one particularly low point, Crook con-
fided to Sheridan that he was "at a loss what to do."[79] The
two commands finally communicated with one another on
July 12 when Privates William Evans, Benjamin F. Stewart,
and James Bell, all of Company E, 7th Infantry, arrived in
Crook's camp bearing dispatches from Terry reporting the
Custer disaster and forecasting probable movement. These
"three cool, determined men, and good shots" had traveled
cross-country from the Yellowstone to Crook at great personal peril, and each was subsequently awarded the Medal of
Honor for his daring.[80]

By midsummer Crook's men had grown somewhat accustomed to frequent pestering raids on their camp by Sioux warriors. Sergeant George Howard of the 2nd Cavalry recorded in his diary on July 10: "We had quite a battle last night, making ten so far this summer. The Indians accomplished nothing but firing the prairie which caused us some trouble."[81] Remarkably, the smoke from that particular prairie fire guided Terry's dispatch carriers directly to Crook's camp. The next evening, the Sioux attacked again. Terry's couriers had just settled in for a badly needed sleep, and they were invited by August Lange, 1st Sgt. of Company H, 9th Infantry, to join in defending the camp. William Evans rolled over and asked his companions, "What do you say, boys, will we go, or take our chances sleeping?" Stewart replied, "Let's go to the next world asleep, if we have to go."[82]

Crook resumed the campaign trail in early August. His Big Horn and Yellowstone Expedition was well reinforced with additional infantry and eight companies of the 5th Cavalry. Those particular troopers were flush from a successful encounter with some Cheyenne who had bolted from Red Cloud Agency in mid-July in an attempt to reach the warring camps. "Revenge for Custer" was the regiment's cry, remembered Danish emigrant Chris Madsen, a private of Company A, when the 5th clashed with the Cheyenne at Warbonnet Creek, Nebraska. There Buffalo Bill Cody killed and scalped a warrior named Yellow Hair. "It was the first scalp for Custer," Madsen recalled, "the first victim of the vengeance which more than anything had been the goal of my regiment."[83] Others of Madsen's company were equally emboldened as they neared Crook. Sergeant John Powers wrote friends back

This stern-looking cavalryman was a friend of Pvt. William N. McDonald, Company B, 6th Infantry, stationed at Fort Abraham Lincoln, Dakota Territory, in the mid-1870s. His four-button blouse was outmoded for 1876, but the wearing of obsolete uniform parts in the field was altogether common and evident in many photos of 1876 soldiers. His pistol is nonregulation and may be a studio prop. B WILLIAM HENRY, JR.

First Sergeant John Ryan, standing, and Sgt. William G. Capes, seated, both of Company M, 7th Cavalry, campaigned against the Sioux in 1876. Ryan played a prominent role in the Little Big Horn battle; Capes was detached from the command and guarded regimental property at the Yellowstone River supply depot, at the mouth of the Powder River. Ryan's detailed and lengthy reminiscence of service with the 7th is one of the most lucid accounts of life in the Old Army and in Custer's famed regiment. GREG MARTIN

The two known soldiers in this setting of 7th Cavalry comrades, Musician George Penwell, Company K, standing at left, and Pvt. Harry A. Abbotts, Company E, seated at left, survived the valley and hilltop fights in the battle of the Little Big Horn. Abbotts had been detailed as an attendant to Dr. James M. DeWolf, who rode with Maj. Marcus Reno and was a casualty in the battle. Abbotts's regularly assigned company rode with Custer and was destroyed.

This photograph of a trim, unnamed private of Company F, 7th Cavalry, was kept in an album maintained by Pvt. William N. McDonald, Company B, 6th Infantry, at Fort Abraham Lincoln, Dakota Territory. Commanded by Capt. George Yates, Company F, the 7th's so-called "Bandbox Troop," was wiped out at the battle of the Little Big Horn. The 7th Cavalry abandoned its sabers at the Powder River Depot in early June 1876, but otherwise this trooper's apparel, including his forage cap and gauntlets, was standard for cavalrymen in the Great Sioux War.
B. WILLIAM HENRY, JR.

Sergeant Benjamin C. Criswell of Company B, 7th Cavalry, was wounded in the hilltop fight at the Little Big Horn. In 1878 he received a Medal of Honor for valor in the battle for recovering the body of 2nd Lt. Benjamin H. Hodgson, a casualty in the valley fight, bringing up ammunition, and encouraging the men in most exposed conditions under heavy fire. He was discharged from the 7th Cavalry in 1878 as a first sergeant of excellent character.
LITTLE BIGHORN BATTLEFIELD NATIONAL MONUMENT

Here Pvt. Gustave Korn, Company I, 7th Cavalry, holds the horse Comanche. Both survived the Little Big Horn. F. Jay Haynes photographed the pair in June 1877 at Fort Abraham Lincoln, with Capt. Henry J. Nowland, the 7th's quartermaster, looking on. A blacksmith, Korn was killed at Wounded Knee on December 29, 1890. Comanche died shortly thereafter. HAYNES FOUNDATION COLLECTION, MONTANA HISTORICAL SOCIETY

No Missouri River steamboat had a more illustrious history than the *Far West,* photographed here by F. Jay Haynes in the late 1870s. Captained in 1876 by the distinguished pilot Grant Marsh, the *Far West* ferried fifty-two wounded 7th Cavalrymen from the mouth of the Little Big Horn River to Fort Abraham Lincoln in a record-setting run never equaled. HAYNES FOUNDATION COLLECTION, MONTANA HISTORICAL SOCIETY

This is one of the .50-caliber Gatling guns that Custer refused to trail to the Little Big Horn. Sergeant Hugh Hynds of Company B, 20th Infantry, left, served on the Gatling detachment during the campaign. Hynds and his comrades here, likely all of the 20th Infantry, were photographed at Fort McKeen, Dakota Territory, in 1877 by F. Jay Haynes of Fargo. HAYNES FOUNDATION COLLECTION, MONTANA HISTORICAL SOCIETY

From his summer studio at the new Fort Keogh, Montana, Stanley J. Morrow of Yankton photographed members of Col. Nelson A. Miles's 5th Infantry in the late 1870s. In 1876 the 5th helped establish Keogh, first known as the Tongue River Cantonment, and tirelessly pursued the Sioux during the later stages of the conflict. This is David W. Page of Company C, 5th Infantry, a participant in the Sioux War surrenders when Sitting Bull's followers returned from Canada in the late 1870s and early 1880s. LARRY NESS

This unnamed 5th Infantryman posing for Stanley Morrow at Fort Keogh in the late 1870s provides a good look at the basic uniform and gear used by infantry troops during the Great Sioux War. Indians particularly feared these foot-bound soldiers, knowing well that their 1873 model Springfield rifles were lethal at distances exceeding one thousand yards. LARRY NESS

Here two doughboys of Nelson Miles's 5th Infantry pose in Stanley Morrow's Fort Keogh studio. Along with otherwise standard mid-1870s apparel, these men wear the new pattern 1876 cartridge belts that reached field troops in mid-1877. A handwritten caption on the back of the photo reads, "Stevens Brothers of Co. F." The man on the right is likely George W. Stevens, who served with Company G in 1876. LARRY NESS

In this scene below Fort Fetterman, Wyoming, reinforcements gather along the North Platte River for field service in Sioux country. This 1876 photograph by D. S. Mitchell of Cheyenne shows troops outbound to either Crook's Big Horn and Yellowstone Expedition or the new army cantonment established on the Powder River near the abandoned Fort Reno, a tattered relic from the Bozeman Trail era. LARRY NESS

Sergeant George S. Howard, Company E, 2nd Cavalry, was a devout diarist and poet who faithfully maintained a splendid account of daily life in Crook's Big Horn and Yellowstone expedition. Proudly known by fellow cavalrymen as "Moccasin Joe—Guide and Hunter," here he was photographed by S. M. Hartwell of Laramie, Wyoming, near the time of his discharge from the army at Fort Sanders in May 1877.
SUSAN C. RENEAU

First Sergeant John Comford of Mackenzie's 4th Cavalry, seen here circa 1876, presents an unusually trim campaign image, having donned a trimmed civilian shirt, flowing silk scarf, and homemade carbine cartridge belt. The use and wearing of nonregulation gear by troops in the field was condoned and even encouraged by superiors. NATIONAL ARCHIVES

Private William Earl Smith, Company E, 4th Cavalry, plainly wears bulky, double-layered clothing, evidence that he and his regiment endured the rigors of a northern plains winter during Crook's Powder River Expedition. Smith fought the Northern Cheyenne in the battle of the Red Fork of the Powder River on November 25, 1876. A lucid diarist, he penned on the back of this image, "sagebrush soldier, one off [*sic*] the boys, 1876." SHERRY L. SMITH

These infantrymen photographed by Stanley Morrow along Whitewood Creek in the northern Black Hills present a haggard but spirited look at the conclusion of the Starvation March. One soldier's irreverence was apparent as he carefully positioned a horseshoe-shaped whiskey flask in the equipment pile in the foreground. The Black Hills provisioners gladly sold spirits to the Regulars. W. H. OVER MUSEUM

Company K, 2nd Cavalry, participated in the Big Horn Expedition in March and Powder River Expedition in November, and spent the summer routinely patrolling the Black Hills Road and responding to Indian raiding throughout southeastern Wyoming. Here photographer D. S. Mitchell documented the outfit on September 16 in Custer City, while escorting Crook to a conference with Sheridan at Fort Laramie. STATE HISTORICAL SOCIETY OF SOUTH DAKOTA

Crook's men passed miners often as they threaded their way through the Black Hills in September 1876. This gold sluicing operation along Whitewood Creek, northeast of Deadwood, was photographed by D. S. Mitchell about when the troops passed. Some soldiers admitted a curiosity about the prospectors and their labors, and Pvt. James Frew of the 5th Cavalry remembered taking his cooking water from such a sluice.
JIM CRAIN

Shooting worn cavalry horses for food was a heartless task, even for infantrymen. Here a doughboy re-creates an altogether common Starvation March occurrence. Yankton photographer Stanley Morrow captured or may even have staged the scene near Custer City in the southern Black Hills, documenting one of the dreadful legacies of soldiering against the Sioux in 1876.
W. H. OVER MUSEUM

These infantrymen of the Big Horn and Yellowstone Expedition illustrate well the rigors of Crook's Starvation March. Their uniforms and equipment are threadbare and worn from arduous marching and nasty weather. Here the doughboys vividly demonstrate for photographer Stanley Morrow their efficiency in butchering a cavalry horse. Such activity was common before the soldiers reached the Black Hills.
PAUL L. HEDREN

Some wounded soldiers from the Little Big Horn and Slim Buttes battles were transported on mule litters like these. This photograph, taken by Stanley Morrow in the southern Black Hills, shows a Slim Buttes soldier being warmed by a plaid civilian blanket and comforted by pine boughs bundled beneath his head and positioned above to cut the sun. LARRY NESS

This bleak-looking camp in the southern Black Hills was photographed by Stanley Morrow on September 30, 1876. The wagons of Crook's Big Horn and Yellowstone Expedition bearing camp equipage had not yet returned from the Big Horn Mountain camp. Here shelters were limited to pine bough wickiups and simple lean-tos, with no particular martial order evident anywhere. PAUL L. HEDREN

The wagons bearing the camp equipage and extraneous personal gear of the Big Horn and Yellowstone Expedition, abandoned when Crook's men struck for the Yellowstone in August 1876, returned to the command in early October while the campaigners recuperated in the southern Black Hills. Loaded with changes of clothing, tentage, and heavy cooking gear, the arrival was warmly welcomed by the men. PAUL L. HEDREN

Here two companies of the 5th Cavalry pause east of Custer City for photographer Stanley Morrow. The lead unit is Company B, commanded by Capt. Robert H. Montgomery. "Montgomery's Grays" participated in the Warbonnet Creek skirmish, Starvation March, and fight at Slim Buttes.

NATIONAL ARCHIVES

These artillery pieces, a three-inch ordnance rifle at left and twelve-pounder Napoleon field gun at right, along with 5th Infantry crews from the Tongue River Cantonment, participated in the Wolf Mountains battle with Crazy Horse's followers on January 8, 1877. This photograph by John H. Fouch was taken on a balmy winter day, evidenced by the soldiers' open coats and wet snow clinging to caisson wheels. JAMES BRUST

Unlike the 7th Cavalry band, which marched with Custer in 1876 as far as the Powder River supply camp, and the 5th Infantry band, which joined its comrades at the Tongue River Cantonment at summer's end, no other bandsmen strayed far from their regimental headquarters during the Great Sioux War. This is Pvt. Henry Christian of the 2nd Cavalry Band, photographed by Stanley J. Morrow at Fort Custer, Montana. Christian's unique muskrat cap was formally authorized by the army in March 1879, though privately purchased fur apparel was widely worn by troops on the northern plains before then. PAUL L. HEDREN

Sergeant Major Alvarado Mortimer Fuller, 2nd Cavalry, was photographed by Stanley Morrow in April 1879 at Fort Custer, Montana. Upon reenlisting in the 2nd Cavalry in April 1876, Fuller was promoted from private to the coveted and singular top sergeant position in the 2nd, supporting his regiment's operations during the Great Sioux War from its headquarters at Fort Sanders, Wyoming. At Fort Custer on June 28, 1879, Fuller was promoted from sergeant major to second lieutenant, Company L, 2nd Cavalry. PAUL L. HEDREN

home that they were finally off to have "some roast Sioux for supper. We were, to believe all accounts, going right down into Mr. Sitting Bull's camp and eat him up without salt."[84] But most other field-hardened troops in the Wyoming and Montana camps did not share such feelings of invincibility.

Crook's return to the trail in August was both arduous and tempered with curiosity. The route down the Tongue River was nightmarish for the infantry, who were forced to cross the stream as many as seventeen times. "The cavalry rode through the water good enough, but the Infantry had to march and wade right through, sometimes breast high, other times knee deep," recalled Corp. John Zimmerman of Company I, 14th Infantry.

> Our first crossing was thought to be our only one, as we had not been told of the others yet; all took off their shoes and stockings, after crossing put them on again and continued the march to the next fording place. At the third crossing, our feet began to get sore from the sharp rocks and sand; we were then told that there were more than a dozen such crossings before us yet for this day, and it would be useless to try to march without keeping our shoes on so after this we marched into the river removing nothing, and not delaying the march, never thinking of changing any more.[85]

Nightly camps could be distinctly painful, too. Private William Jordan, also of the 14th Infantry, wrote in his diary: "I spread my blanket out on what I thought was a nice patch of grass, but it turned out to be an ant hill, and I had no more than settled myself for a few hours' rest when I felt about a dozen of the most excruciating bites on my body and legs. We never disrobe when following the trail of Indians, and the ants had crawled in under my clothing and next to the skin in a way that made me wince."[86] Incessant rains also tormented the troops. On August 12, 1876, Jordan wrote: "Has rained steadily for forty-eight hours. In camp. No shelter of any kind. Stood up all night with blankets over our shoulders, and soaking wet. One soldier proved an exception. Name, Andy Shuttles. First man I ever saw who could lie down in a pool of water, with water dammed up against his back and running over him, and sleep like a top."[87] Rain tormented some men in yet another way. Remembered 7th Cavalryman Ami Mulford: "We have no change of clothing now, so will have to get dry as best we can, and the best way is to roll up in your saddle blanket and sweat it out, all the time getting full benefit of the aroma that arises from the sweat from your horse's sides and back, as it creeps up out of the blanket."[88]

In Montana, Crook's men observed pronounced Indian trails, of which many diarists paid particular attention. Private James Frew of the 5th Cavalry recorded the command's discovery of a "very heavy Indian trail. Like a road."[89] Doughboy Howard thought the Indian trail looked like a "big square . . . they having wounded warriors on travois."[90] As to the probability of these or any trails actually leading soldiers to Indians, 2nd Cavalryman William Zimmer may have captured reality best: "You might as well hunt a needle in a haystack, as to hunt Indians in small parties."[91]

Crook's trail down Rosebud Creek took his men past Indian graves and a large Sun Dance camp from the previous June. "Went past several rather fresh Indian graves and the remains of a large shed where a large Sundance had been held," recorded Howard. "There were six buffalo Heads collected in the ring and a War pole in the center smeared with blood."[92] Custer's men had passed the same Indian camp on June 24, and diarists in that column noted the same buffalo heads and pole.[93]

Many soldiers took pleasure in looting Indian graves, on the Rosebud and wherever encountered during the long course of the Great Sioux War. Stanislas Roy of Company A remembered passing graves in trees along the Yellowstone before the 7th Cavalry began its push to the Little Big Horn. "G troop men tore them down and robbed them and threw bones into [the] Yellowstone. Some of the men told McIntosh that G troop might be sorry for this."[94] In the Little Big Horn village, soldiers absconded with buffalo robes and blankets swaddling Indian dead, some of those wraps becoming bedding for Reno's wounded men. There, as well, 1st Lt. Gustavus Doane of the 2nd Cavalry collected several pairs of moccasins. Dr. Holmes Paulding fancied a pair of moccasins with beaded soles, but the offensive odor and the adhesion of skin that slipped away from the flesh as he tugged them off caused him to quit his thieving. Trooper William White boasted of taking a half dozen pairs of moccasins from village graves, and also a hand mirror, but then groused when someone else stole the moccasins from him at one of the Yellowstone River camps.[95]

Given the opportunity, the enlisted men, like their officers, proved to be adept pothunters, especially when passing through abandoned Indian camps. Private Thompson set out to get trophies from the Little Big Horn village, but instead found blood-soaked stone hammers and evidently lost his lust for collecting.[96] Private William Smith of the 4th Cavalry was less hesitant when rooting through Morning Star's village on the Red Fork of the Powder River on November 25, 1876. There he was particularly enamored with a catlinite pipe, but he had to first wrestle it away from an aged Indian woman whose tepee he was ransacking.[97] Private Ami Mulford, a Custer Avenger campaigning with the 7th Cavalry in the summer of 1877, joined fellow soldiers in thoroughly exploring Sitting Bull's sacked village at the head of Cedar Creek, north of the Yellowstone. This camp had been abandoned when attacked by Col. Nelson Miles's command on the preceding October 21. Lying about were scores of tepee poles, pegged buffalo hides, paints and charms, aged firearms, axes marked with the letters "U.S.Q.M.D.," and even a coffee mill, its drawer containing cloth bags of beads and herbs.[98]

A surprisingly large number of enlisted men found the collecting of agates, petrified wood, and fossils fascinating. The Yellowstone country was, and is still, noted for a distinctive variety of moss agate, and the men delighted in scavenging the gravelly watercourses and hillsides for these dreamy gems. It is difficult imagining beleaguered soldiers trucking weighty stones in their haversacks and saddlebags, but collecting proved a welcome diversion that many soldiers commented on.[99] Not everyone was charmed, however. Private William Jordan's company commander groused about the way in which the "boys fell out of column to gather these curiosities," and he declared sarcastically that "we [were] not making a geological survey."[100]

Crook and Terry united their commands in the waning days of August and desperately sought direction for their demoralized campaigners. Their men, meanwhile, settled into yet another routine of daily camp life, surrounded by increasing numbers of soldiers, the diverse opportunities of the Yellowstone River, and the proximity of steamboats and sutlers.

The men particularly seized opportunities on the Yellowstone to bathe and wash clothes. Bathing on campaign was a welcome indulgence, even in the Yellowstone's chilly waters. Earlier in the campaign, Private Jordan recorded the misadventure of a company comrade, Pat Robinson:

> The day being hot and the march a long one, the men were tired and footsore, and, on striking camp, they were soon busy bathing their feet in various water holes in the dry bed of the river. Robinson was careful to select a choice hole near the bank, and was all prepared to bathe his tired extremities, when the mules that had been unhooked and turned out to graze came along and drank all the water out of Pat's hole, leaving him high and dry on the bank. The language he used at the time came near drying up all the other holes.[101]

When 5th Cavalryman James Frew washed his threadbare shirt on September 22 in Spring Creek in the northern Black

Hills, he quipped in his diary that he'd had no change of clothing since August 4.[102]

Whether on the Yellowstone in midsummer 1876 or on the frozen Wyoming prairie in December, the always unpredictable northern plains weather plagued the campaigners incessantly. Either it was too hot or "cold & windy" in summer,[103] or it was so cold in winter that thermometers congealed. Recalled 1st Sgt. James McClellan of Company H, 3rd Cavalry, of December 24, 1876: "Thermometer went down to forty-two below zero and froze. Had to melt snow to make coffee. This is the coldest we have had yet, in fact I do not know how cold it was as we could not tell, the mercury having frozen."[104]

Snakes and bugs tormented the troops, too. Clearing new campsites of rattlesnakes became a diligent afternoon routine, and bites were not uncommon.[105] Mosquitoes often plagued the men as well, Sergeant Howard grousing about them on Goose Creek, Wyoming, and Sgt. John Cox of the 1st Infantry calling those swarming the Yellowstone-Missouri confluence at Fort Buford the fiercest "of any place in the Union."[106] Even grasshoppers stymied the campaigners. Mulford recalled: "They chewed holes in our tents, blankets, overcoats, etc., and one of the men lost thirty rounds of ammunition, and when questioned as to what had become of it, he said that the grasshoppers had eaten it, brass shells and all."[107]

A phenomenon new to the men of Crook's Big Horn and Yellowstone Expedition was the presence of steamboats on the Yellowstone. Crook's troops had come from the land of railroads and wagons, but they now had entered the realm of these powerful river craft. The men particularly noticed the manner in which Terry's command relied on boats to move their "needfuls," as Private Howard called the camp equipage. In early August 1876 no less than seven boats plied the Yellowstone, augmenting a subsistence and quartermaster train of two hundred wagons.[108] By then, Crook had long since abandoned his wagon train and was supporting his soldiers off the backs of pack mules. The scene repeated itself in 1877. Mulford of the 7th Cavalry wrote: "[We could] see and hear the steamboats on the Missouri and Yellowstone rivers, so do not consider we are entirely out of the world. There are thirty-eight different steamers on the upper Missouri this Summer."[109]

Small packet boats like the *Josephine, Carroll,* and *Silver Lake* delivered supplies and reinforcements, particularly to the combined Terry-Gibbon command; ferried soldiers to and fro; and brought sutlers to the Yellowstone. "Sutlers [were] a curse to the army," cracked Private Coleman of the 7th Cavalry, recalling that they sold whiskey and charged exorbitant prices for everything.[110] But they also peddled fresh vegetables, a tantalizing array of canned and bottled goods, tobacco, clothing, and even writing paper. One trader's credit ledger survives, but of 131 customers accounted for, barely twenty-five were enlisted men, clerks, and teamsters, and certainly only those the trader might expect to see again.[111] Cash trade dominated the business, but that, too, limited the enlisted men. And even when common soldiers had cash, stocks were not always bountiful or fresh. Remembered Mulford: "Bought a dozen eggs. They turned out to be condensed chickens, but the sutler charged the small sum of one dollar and twenty-five cents for them just the same."[112] Writing in his diary on August 20, 1876, Private Sanford was equally disillusioned: "Took a walk

over to our old camp ground and to the Sutlers, but he had
... nothing to sell but tin ware."[113]

Occasionally a certain gaiety pervaded the well-scattered
camp circles along the Yellowstone and elsewhere in Sioux
country. Singing was a popular relaxation at evening camp-
fires, the men enjoying religious, sentimental, and comic
songs, and especially scripted and made-up verses of the popular Harrigan and Hart ballad "The Regular Army O."[114] As
well, the men played cards, shared stories of home and adventure, and indulged in an array of athletic games and sports,
including baseball.[115] When opportunity allowed, the men
adopted pets of all sorts. Private William Jordan of the 14th
Infantry wrote of the occasion in mid-August 1876 when
Capt. Andrew Burt of the 9th Infantry adopted a stray Indian
dog he named Sitting Bull, but Burt's dog scrapped with
Capt. Thomas Tobey's dog, Walloper, and soon deserted the
camp.[116] Sanford remembered the diverse pets in the Yellowstone River supply camps: "Eagles, owls, crows, Horned toads,
[and] queer rats like a kangaroo."[117]

Perhaps the greatest camp and trail pleasure was derived
from receiving mail and newspapers. Quipped Howard in his
diary: "It seems very good to hear from civilization once
more."[118] Even in the harshest of conditions, news from
home brightened a soldier's day. Said 1st Sgt. James McClellan
of the 3rd Cavalry, marching in Crook's wintertime Powder
River Expedition: "Snow all day but got a good mail which
makes up for all this."[119]

Some soldiers vented pent-up emotion and angst in
poetry, usually in the form of scattered lines committed to

their private diaries. But in at least one instance, a doughboy's verse was forwarded to the nearest newspaper, the *Cheyenne Daily Leader.* Musician Timothy Burns of Company K, 4th Infantry, present with his outfit guarding the Black Hills stage road at the mouth of Red Canyon, Dakota, in the summer of 1876, penned an epitaph for Custer titled "Custer and His Band." The poem captured both the emotional pangs of loss and the soldiers' ardent desire for retribution.

> Sleep on ye brave and sainted dead,
> Ye gallant fallen few;
> In a daring charge your blood was shed,
> By the treacherous, savage Sioux.
> That martial soul who led your band
> Through the foemen's raking fire,
> Has soared aloft to that heavenly land,
> To join the angels choir.
>
> Rest on, brave band, the nation keeps
> Your regard in her breast,
> In bloody scrolls 'tis written there,
> Your deeds and names caressed;
> And ere September's sun doth set
> Ten thousand blades shall leap
> To avenge the gallant Custer's death,
> Where his chiefs and comrades sleep.
>
> That holy ground, where sleeps the brave
> Shall never be forgot.

> The prairie winds sigh o'er the grave
> In glory guards the spot.
> Their noble souls have gone to rest,
> They've heard their last tattoo;
> Their mem'ries will be ever blest
> By their brothers in the blue.[120]

As recognized national holidays came and went, not all commands celebrated. Private Thomas Coleman of the 7th Cavalry recalled the melancholy Fourth of July in Terry's camp on the Yellowstone, just below the mouth of the Big Horn River. "There is nothing to distinguish it from any other day. No firing of artillery, no speech making, no demonstration whatever, not even a drunken man around camp. Everything quiet and everybody wrapped in his own thoughts and a great many in their blankets. How different it is in civilized country."[121] Downstream at the mouth of the Powder River, however, the companions of Corp. Samuel Meddaugh of the 6th Infantry torched a large woodpile atop Sheridan's Butte, across the Yellowstone from their camp. The men celebrated the nation's centennial and called the blaze their "Fourth of July bonfire," said Meddaugh. "It made a fine sight against the sky, and no doubt could be seen for many miles, much to the wonder of the Indians who may have seen it."[122]

Thanksgiving Day meant little to the field-bound men of Crook's Powder River Expedition. "We had a regular old thanksgiving dinner [consisting of] bacon and flapjacks," lamented Pvt. William Smith of the 4th Cavalry. "Not much running around today."[123] Smith's diary entry on December

25 was equally woeful: "We had a regular old Christmas dinner. A little piece of fat bacon and hard tack and a half cup of coffee. You bet I thought of home now if I ever did."[124]

Despite the occasional presence of whiskey in the camps and the rambunctiousness that could arise in idle men, discipline was maintained in the ranks both subtly and overtly. Once when men of Ranald Mackenzie's 4th Cavalry failed to show proper respect to their commanding officer, the colonel called a sergeant and instructed him to take the offending soldiers to the edge of camp and make them salute a stump for an hour and a half.[125] On the Yellowstone, two men of the 2nd Cavalry tangled with trader's liquor and aroused the ire of their noncommissioned officers. Remembered Private Zimmer: "Mr. Q. got his ear broke by the corporal for refusing some duty and Mr. H. was riding his horse around like some Irish duke. He got tied up to a cottonwood tree for three hours to freeze sober." [126]

Malingerers were irksome, too. After a hard day's march with Crook in early August 1876, many infantry dropped from the ranks, exhausted, and were carried to the evening camp on the pack mules. But one soldier who was not sick also sought transportation to camp. Dr. Julius H. Patzki caught on to the ruse and at first talked very kindly to the faker, even offering to carry the man's rifle and ammunition on his horse. When the man was unarmed, however, Patzki "turned . . . on the soldier and began prodding him along at the point of the bayonet. He started him off on the double quick and kept him moving until he rejoined his company, where he was placed under guard, but later released."[127]

Desertions were not infrequent, especially when the various field commands were within reasonable distances of beckoning communities. Perhaps the strangest Great Sioux War desertion occurred on the Yellowstone at the end of July 1876. While camped at the mouth of Big Porcupine Creek, just upstream from the Rosebud, Corp. Samuel Meddaugh of the roving 6th Infantry depot guard recorded watching "three men going down the Yellowstone in a small boat. We ordered them ashore, but they refused to stop, and Major Moore sent scouts to stop them, but without success."[128]

These companies of Col. Ranald Mackenzie's 4th Cavalry were photographed in early August 1876 by D. S. Mitchell near the Eagle's Nest, a landmark southwest of Fort Laramie. The regiment was en route to Fort Laramie and Camp Robinson, first intending to replace the 5th Cavalry as guardians of gold field roads and traffic in the southern Black Hills, and then serving as the principal mounted complement in Crook's fall Powder River Expedition.

JIM CRAIN

4

To Horse

THE UNNATURAL ORDER OF STEAMBOATS, TRADERS, BASEBALL games, and the ungainly combined field commands ended in late August 1876, when the various columns separated, with Miles establishing a headquarters for his new Yellowstone Command at the mouth of the Tongue River, Terry and Gibbon shortly closing their summer campaigns and guiding their troops to home stations, and Crook determined to resume the chase at any cost. Already the men of his Big Horn and Yellowstone Expedition were hardened to the field in ways different from Terry's and Gibbon's soldiers. "[We went] east with only a spoon, tin cup and knife," remembered Sergeant Howard of the 14th Infantry.[129] Corporal Zimmerman of Howard's regiment recalled their fate similarly: "Each man had one quart cup, no other cooking utensil, he toasted his bacon or ate it raw. Boiled his coffee in the cup and drank it from the same, making it strong or weak as far as the coffee would go."[130] Private Alfred McMachin of Company E, 5th Cavalry, remembered a fellow veteran's quip: "When the pack train starts out look out for hard times."[131] The portending prophesy of an excruciating fall campaign revealed itself even in the first days away from the Yellowstone. Groused Sergeant Howard: "Cold. No Blankets, no tent and clothing soaked. What a miserable life."[132]

Rain pummeled Crook's men for twenty-six consecutive days as they marched eastward across the tortured Little Missouri badlands and then southward across the barren Dakota prairie toward the Black Hills. The men foraged the land when the opportunity allowed. Corporal Zimmerman mentioned feasting on wild plums with his fellow doughboys, and Private Frew of the 5th Cavalry wrote of stewing buffalo berries gathered from the banks of the Little Missouri River.[133] Private O. C. Pollock, Company M, 3rd Cavalry, remembered the bleak Dakota badlands as nothing more than "alkali, sand and water, no wood, only rosebuds, choke cherries and wild plums for a few days, when even they ceased, and left only alkali and needle grass."[134] "Shortly after this came the commencement of our hard times," recalled Zimmerman, "as we were notified that our rations were running short, and must expect to live on half rations and probably less. . . . A few days of short rations soon whets up the appetite."[135]

After the troops crossed the Little Missouri, their daily food allowance amounted to two hard crackers, a half ration of coffee, an occasional bite of a foraged deer, and such reserved tidbits as individual soldiers had tucked into their haversacks or saddlebags. "In their tired and famished condition, great disaffection existed among the soldiers, and the necessity of living on half-rations was freely discussed," grumbled Private McMachin of the 5th Cavalry.[136]

Before the expedition's rations were entirely exhausted, however, a handful of soldiers successfully thieved some beans from one of the packers—*and* General Crook. Packer David Mears concluded to have a breakfast "blow-out" with the last beans available in the pack train, and he invited Crook to the "grand mess." As the beans cooked through the evening, lingering soldiers pestered the packer's cook, offering $20 for the beans. Mears learned of the offer but admonished the cook not to sell for any money, as he had invited Crook and his staff for breakfast. But the next morning, the beans were gone stolen. Said Mears: "The cook swore that he did not sell them, neither did he eat them, but I will always think that cook got what he could eat and sold the balance."[137]

Two weeks into the march, many men were nearing starvation, and orders passed through the command to shoot played-out mules and cavalry horses for issue as beef. Private Thomas Lloyd of Company E, 3rd Cavalry, wrote to his cousin:

> I don't mind the fighting part, but the hardships we had to go through and the starvation. You would likely think it rather hard to sit down and eat horse meat for your dinner at home. . . . But, what do you think of me and everyone else, as soon as you would get to camp, shoot an old sore back mule, so poor that he could hardly walk, take your butcher knife, cut as nice a slice as you could get and eat it raw. No salt, pepper nor anything at all, live on it for eight days and travel from twenty to forty miles a day.[138]

Complaining was widespread. "This is a fine food for men in a civilized country," groused Sergeant Howard of the 2nd Cavalry.[139] Other soldiers accepted their humble fate. "Although no salt was issued to the command the men appeared to eat the meat with great relish," remembered Pvt. Richard Flynn of Company D, 4th Infantry. On September 8, "the broiling and roasting was kept up all night and the morrow's rations [were] consumed at once before the men [were] satisfied," he added.[140]

On September 8 Crook hurried 150 well-mounted cavalrymen southward to the Black Hills to procure foodstuffs for his desperate command, and on the ninth this makeshift battalion chanced upon a Sioux village nestled in the sheltering, pine-covered Slim Buttes in the northwestern corner of today's South Dakota. Soon the entire command was engaged. The villagers were easily routed, and the men gathered foodstuffs in the camp, consisting mostly of dried buffalo meat and berries, and distributed them to the famished soldiers. The men also received their daily allotment of horse meat. Flynn remembered how the dried Indian meat, "being somewhat fat helped greatly to cook the horse meat and make it more palatable."[141]

As some campaigners were prone to do, the soldiers explored the Indian village to satisfy their innate curiosity. Buffalo robes were abundant, recalled Sergeant Howard, and the lodges were made of the finest tanned buffalo skins. "We found a great many articles used in civilization, among the collection almost every article used by the housewife in the kitchen and a great many things recognized as belonging to the 7th Cavalry showing that those Indians had been in that fight."[142] A particularly diligent scrounger from the 5th Cavalry remembered finding a locket, a picture of Captain Keogh, two gold-mounted ivory-handled revolvers, and a Spencer sporting rifle. "The picture and locket I gave to an officer of Third Cavalry, who claimed them as a relative of the officer killed with Custer, and a revolver I gave to Captain Rodgers of Company A, 5th Cavalry. The rifle I sold some days later for two loaves of bread."[143] Finding 7th Cavalry relics associated with the Little Big Horn battle here and in other Indian villages became for some combatants a justifying comfort that balanced their own privation and continuing casualties with a belief that they were exacting retribution for that horrendous disaster.

Crook incurred three casualties at Slim Buttes, and these dead received a much more careful interment than Terry and Gibbon had accorded Custer's men. Corporal Zimmerman documented the burial in his journal: "A large hole was dug in the ground right in the main trail, all of them laid in it, covered with their blankets, then with canvass, filling up the hole as neatly as possible. A fire was then built on top of this, the ashes afterward scattered out about the place, all the command, horses and men then marched over the spot, obliterating all signs of breaking the earth."[144]

A similar interment after Mackenzie's fight with Morning Star was equally bleak. Remembered Private Smith of the 4th Cavalry: "In the afternoon we went to bury the dead and it was the hardest looking funeral I was ever at. Well, we got it done. . . . I just thought then I would never like to be left in the ground in this wild country where no white man would ever see the place again. The way they bury in this country, they take and sew a man up in a blanket and don't have no coffin."[145] An even humbler interment had occurred in the hurried abandonment of Old Bear's village on the Powder River the previous March 17. Old Bear's Cheyenne had been attacked by troops commanded by Col. Joseph Reynolds, and in the aftermath, two casualties received what Private Pollock of the 3rd Cavalry labeled a "soldier burial." "A hole was cut in the ice, which was two feet thick, and they were given a cold bath, head on."[146]

The privation endured by Crook's men in the week before the Slim Buttes battle paled compared with that on the several subsequent days. The cold, wet weather chilled the men to the core. Mud clung to soles of their boots, shoes, and horses' hooves, doubling the travails of their closing march to the Black Hills. Private Frew remembered how sore-backed cavalry horses were at a discount for a while, so long as there were Indian ponies to eat. But the ponies lasted barely a day. Whatever the type, the horses, he said, "were eaten up clean, even the heart, liver, and lights, and not a bit of salt." Some soldiers used cartridge powder to season the meat.[147] "We were not growing fat by any means," quipped Corporal Zimmerman of the 14th Infantry. "Our meat was all gone except a few strips of dried buffalo, no bread, no crackers, no coffee, no sugar, bacon long since disappeared, nothing but the water of the prairie, as we had any amount of rain. Bread, bread, anything would be paid for bread," the men lamented.[148]

No less a personal privation than the foul weather and scant rations was the want of tobacco, the "weed that a soldier likes even better than he does whiskey," remembered Private Coleman of the 7th Cavalry.[149] Zimmerman wrote that a "miserable quid of tobacco was quite a solace to many a soldier on the march. . . . It was a common thing for one soldier to offer another twenty dollars for a small piece . . . yet this would not buy it, much less any bread or crackers."[150] In weak moments, some men smoked coffee grounds and prairie grass.[151]

By September 12, 1876, the privation of Crook's march nearly destroyed his command. Fifth Cavalryman Alfred McMachin wrote to friends in Hays, Kansas: "It was pitiful and heart-rending to see the sufferings of the Infantry and the dismounted portion of the Cavalry, dragging their weary limbs over the muddy trail. I saw that day soldiers who were a short time previously strong men, sit down by the trail in despair, large, bitter tears running down their emaciated cheeks, being exhausted from starvation and long marches."[152] "The men were falling out of the ranks from sheer exhaustion. For miles the trail was strewn with played-out men and horses, cavalry saddles, blankets, each trooper abandoning his traps in order to lighten the burden of his patient and faithful horse," wrote 14th Infantryman William Jordan in his daily diary. "Had the Indians known of our weak condition they would have had an opportunity to avenge themselves for the thrashing we gave them at Slim Buttes."[153]

Remembered Zimmerman:

Our camp this night [September 12] was only a lay down on the bare ground, many being too weak to look for blankets and unable to carry them if they

found them. During the whole night we heard strag-
glers coming into camp, trying to find their companions. Our first sergeant, when about five miles from
camp, fell down and could go no farther. He told me
that if we got to camp safe, to come back after him
in the morning and bring him in dead or alive. He
with some others made a final start, and struggled
into camp before morning, but hundreds of them did
not arrive until late next day. Many had to be
brought in on pack mules.[154]

"The suffering of this command will not soon be forgotten by those who unfortunately belonged to it," wrote
McMachin.[155]

For these Great Sioux War veterans, and quickly for all
Regular army men, Crook's "Starvation March" in September
1876 became another of the defining episodes of the conflict,
and ultimately of the Trans-Mississippi Indian wars. The
cumulative deprivation brought on by having no wagon support, no shelter, foul weather, cold camps, and diminished
rations supplemented by horse meat was compounded by
long daily marches across an arduous and bleak landscape and
then an occasional adrenaline-charged Indian fight. The experience was endured but never forgotten by the twenty-two
hundred officers and enlisted men of the Big Horn and Yellowstone Expedition, and by some of the men it was never
forgiven. "I have never heard Crook's name mentioned but
with a curse," 5th Cavalryman James Frew wrote to his father
as the command recuperated in the Black Hills.[156]

The humbling Starvation March ended at about midday on September 13, after the command had trudged five more miles to the Belle Fourche River in the shadow of the Black Hills. There thirteen wagons of provisions from Crook City awaited the men. "Oh! Glad tiding of great joy," scrawled McMachin. "The weary soldier retired to his hard couch, but not supperless."[157] The wagons delivered bacon, coffee, flour, and sugar in bulk, along with every canned eatable that could be procured in Deadwood and Crook City. Drovers pushed cattle, which were butchered and distributed immediately. "Rations were issued tonight and the greatest portion of the command remained up all night cooking and feasting," penned 4th Infantryman Richard Flynn. And for the first time in thirteen days, on the fourteenth the weather turned favorable, "enabling the men to dry their bedding and clean their clothes."[158]

Crook's men celebrated again on October 4, 1876, when their wagon train, long since abandoned in northern Wyoming, rejoined them. "Great joy was manifested by the men on receiving their clothing and extra bedding in which they stood in great need of. The mail which had accumulated during the absence of the command from the train was also brought and distributed," remembered 4th Infantryman Flynn. He also noted, however, the continuing mortality of the hard campaign. "One man of the Fifth Cavalry and two of the Second Cavalry [were] buried today having died of typhoid fever, four more cases being in the hospital."[159]

Of the Black Hills settlements and luring gold fields that in such large measure had precipitated the Great Sioux

War, only Privates James Frew and Daniel Brown of the 5th Cavalry offered comments in their writings. Frew admitted to some curiosity about mining. He had obtained his cooking water one day from a mining sluice, and while there he watched the miners "washing gold." Evidently he tried his hand at panning too, but at best "found [only] some rubies."[160] Brown, of Company G, was more cynical. According to the newspapers, the Black Hills were a place where one returned "in a short time a millionaire," he wrote. "I find this illusion dispelled from practical illustration by the number of tramps returning from the Hills broken in spirit and in pocket."[161]

The worn and haggard appearance of Crook's command evident in the many Stanley Morrow photographs taken in September and October 1876 was in great measure the result of the soldiers' recent ordeal, but hard campaigning took a toll on men, uniforms, and equipment everywhere.[162] Recalled Private Pollock of the 3rd Cavalry: "[We were] as homely, ragged, and sassy a bunch of U.S. Regulars (or, as we were called by the prospectors in the Black Hills, 'Blue Bellies'), as one could have found even in the trenches in No Man's Land."[163] In his reminiscences, Pvt. William White of Company F, 2nd Cavalry, commented about the uniforms in Gibbon's Montana Column:

> Our . . . outfit . . . presented very little appearance that we were United States soldiers. To a distant observer it would have been excusable to regard us as an organized horde of bandits. Only an occasional one of us had remaining on his body some article of the standard Army uniform. . . . Many ragged or

worn-out or discarded blouses or trousers that had been new when we left Fort Ellis on the first day of April were supplanted by checkered "hickory" shirts or overalls, or both. Army hats and caps had been lost, some to be substituted by handkerchiefs or rags tied over heads, while in other cases the loser went bareheaded. Boots or shoes battered to worthlessness had been thrown away, while crude moccasins made of buffalo skin or other skin took their place on soldier feet. Uncut hair and shaggy beards were in universal vogue.[164]

White also remembered the uniforming paradox when new recruits arrived on the Yellowstone. "In every way they presented the spick-and-span snappiness of military style. Our people looked, in comparison, like a band of ragamuffins. Major Brisbin, our leader, was not any better clad than the average of us. He was not even wearing his insignia of rank."[165] Crook was especially renowned in military circles for his comfortably disheveled appearance, an impression remembered by a number of campaign veterans and observers. Packer Henry Daly recalled:

In a populous place General Crook would have worn the regulation uniform, but it probably would have needed pressing. A battered slouch hat would have been carelessly thrust on his head and his boots would have been dusty. In the field, except that everyone knew him, General Crook might have been taken for a Montana miner. The only part of

the uniform he wore was an old overcoat. Except in
wet weather he wore moccasins, and his light, bushy
beard would be gathered in a series of braids.[166]

At Fort Laramie in mid-September 1876, Crook, having
relinquished his command to hurry forward to confer with
Sheridan, was sought by a newspaperman. When the reporter
was unable to distinguish the general in the Fort Laramie
officers' club, he returned to the trader's store and again
inquired about him. The clerk asked him, "Did you see a
large man with a full beard dressed in canvas hunting clothes
and a slouch hat?"

"Yes," replied the reporter, "I saw a seedy looking man
dressed as you describe, but I am looking for General Crook."

"That's him," replied the clerk.

"Well," said the reporter, "I took that man to be one of
the bosses of a mule train."[167]

Uniform conditions were hardly any better in 1877.
Custer Avenger Ami Mulford of the 7th Cavalry was amazed
at "how unkempt the soldiers were—unshaven, uniforms
flayed and dirty; many with their hair nearly down to their
collars; gaunt and hungry-looking, yet, withal, as good and
jolly a lot of men as I ever met."[168]

Though the enlisted men fighting the Great Sioux War
offered little commentary on their reasons for taking the field
in 1876 and 1877, they demonstrated less restraint in critiquing their officers and expressing attitudes at the closures
of the various campaigns. Crook was especially reviled by the

common soldiers in his command. In the wake of the Rose-
bud fight in mid-June 1876, Sergeant Howard of the 2nd
Cavalry thought the fight was "poorly conducted. The sol-
diers have lost all confidence in General Crook."[169] Private
McMachin of the 5th Cavalry was sharply critical of Crook's
September operation, labeling the campaign a "disaster, and a
depletion of the public purse," and adding, "Custer and his
three hundred brave soldiers still remain unavenged, and the
Indian Question is further from solution than ever."[170] Major
Reno, too, was roundly criticized by many in his command.
Private Thompson of Company E, 7th Cavalry, labeled
Reno's conduct "cowardly in the extreme. His refusal to
allow Captain Weir of Company D to go to Custer's relief
when he begged permission, and his own inaction goes to
show his incapability."[171] The following summer, Private Mulford of the 7th Cavalry expressed equal displeasure with Lt.
Col. Elwell Otis of the 22nd Infantry, operating under Miles's
Yellowstone Command. Wrote Mulford: "It strikes me as
rather queer that Colonel Otis should devote so much time
to visiting abandoned Indian village sites instead of getting in
actual contact with hostiles."[172]

On the other hand, Capt. Frederick Benteen earned
warm praise from Thompson and Pvt. William Taylor of Company A for coolness and valor under fire at the Little Big
Horn. Wrote Thompson: "I saw Captain Benteen hard at work
placing a few men here and a few there. He was [as] cool and
collected as ever. I noticed that blood was making its way
through the leg of his trousers and I concluded that he had
received a flesh wound, but with the exception of a slight limp
he gave no signs of pain. His presence was cheering and

encouraging to the men. Wherever he went, their faces lighted up with hope."[173] And according to Taylor, Benteen was "one of the bravest acting men of our entire command."[174]

As for the war generally, an unnamed 5th Infantry enlisted man penned a sentiment that seemed widely embraced among soldiers, enlisted and commissioned alike. Writing of an incident at the Fort Peck Agency in the winter of 1876, the doughboy observed:

> The soldiers became acquainted with the faces of many of the hostiles, and here again met them strolling freely and leisurely about this government agency with Henry rifles; saw one present his ration ticket and get his seven rations, a state of affairs such as was never before recorded in the history of government. While these government troops were out enduring all the rigor of this frigid clime, while making long, toilsome, difficult marches, here were the Indians, for the punishment of whom all this endurance and labor were undergone, comfortably sheltered and protected, some fed and clad by a branch of the government. We want, partially at least, fair play. We don't mind fighting against odds, but in the manner of endurance of this climate the Indians, having had a life-long training, and thereby having a great advantage, should be kept out while troops are out.[175]

Private John McBlain of Company L, 2nd Cavalry, wrote that the generals "chased and followed [the Indians] back and forth across the Yellowstone about a dozen times, keeping them constantly on the move, giving them no rest until they found it to their advantage to go into the agencies and live off the bountiful provision made for them by our merciful and forgiving government."[176] This lament about the "fight them in summer and feed them in winter" policy was heard at Red Cloud Agency, too, and was one of the frank and timeless realities of the American Indian wars.[177]

At the close of the various campaigns against the Sioux and their allies in 1876 and 1877, some enlisted men offered parting commentary. In his diary, 4th Infantryman Richard Flynn offered this causal note: "The Expedition upon its arrival at this post [Camp Robinson, Nebraska] was discontinued and the several companies composing it were ordered to their respective stations. Total distance marched by the company with the Big Horn and Yellow Stone Expedition in the year of [the] Lord 1876 Twelve Hundred (1260) Sixty Miles."[178] Upon returning to his station, 2nd Cavalry Sgt. George Howard, a four-year veteran soldier, wrote: "Arrived at Fort Sanders November 4th after being eight months and nineteen days in the saddle. Twenty-six hundred miles, a pretty fair summer campaign."[179] Corporal John Zimmerman of the 14th Infantry, serving in his second five-year enlistment in 1876, penned a reminiscence ten years later and offered perhaps the most thought-provoking summary:

This ended the worst campaign I ever experienced, and the sequel to this will make as much of a history as I have already written. Such campaigns do not show their effects until years afterward and today out of forty men to a company, I can only find three that were in that long and arduous march after Sitting Bull. . . . Many of them vowed that they would never be caught on another campaign.[180]

These weather-beaten privates of the 5th Cavalry were survivors of Crook's infamous Starvation March and the Slim Buttes action. Dressed in the versatile garb of field service, they are, left to right, Richard L. Davis, Company C; August Schneider, Company C; John R. Jones, Company G; Frederick Sutcliffe, Company C; and Lewis C. Boone, Company C. The image was likely taken in Custer City in late September or October 1876, when photographer Stanley J. Morrow worked the gold fields and documented troop movements. JEROME A. GREENE

5

Tattoo

IN THEIR VARIOUS DIARIES, LETTERS, AND REMINISCENCES, THE enlisted veterans of the Great Sioux War speak with amazing clarity on the conflict, framing a compelling commoners' perspective on an extraordinary saga for the American Army. While, indeed, officers studied the maps, commanded the battlefields, and often enjoyed canned oysters and tomatoes on the campaign trail, these enlisted men subordinated themselves to an inglorious and dangerous routine, eating trail dust and horse meat, trading the next month's wages for a quid of tobacco, rejoicing over the simple pleasures of changing into dry socks and clean underwear, and paying the utmost respect to fallen comrades.

In many ways, this conflict with the Sioux shared traits in common with most other western Indian wars. Whether on a campaign in the 1850s, '60s, or '70s, the trails were always long and dusty. Daily field rations were invariably poor in quality, meager in quantity, and lacking in variety. And while finding and fighting the enemy was the universal goal, that native foe was always remarkably elusive, and contact with him was extraordinarily dangerous. At best, for some veterans of the 1876–77 conflict, their lone distinguishing boast was that this was *their* war.

To be sure, however, the Great Sioux War had its defining moments. To somehow have been at the Little Big Horn in the final week of June 1876, whether a battle casualty, a survivor, or among the relief corps, was to have earned immediate and lasting status in the annals of American military and social history, as revered as participation in the Gettysburg campaign and the Normandy D-Day invasion were to other generations of American soldiers. Similarly, to have survived the inglorious Starvation March in September 1876 was to have earned time-honored respect in the Old Army so long as the traditions of the horse cavalry and Indian campaigns survived. Even before the Great Sioux War concluded, when rations fell short and times were tough, the campaigners honored the travails of Crook's men who stayed their march despite horrendous personal privation.[181]

In the years following the war, its Regular army veterans gradually melted into American society. Many soldiers, like Medal of Honor–winning messenger Pvt. Benjamin Stewart of the 7th Infantry, took discharges upon the expiration of their enlistments and embarked for untold new adventures, whether on farm or ranch, in the industrial cities of the East, or in the ever-enticing mining camps of the West. First Sergeant John Ryan took his discharge from the 7th Cavalry at Fort Rice in December 1876, subsequently becoming a policeman and raising a family in West Newton, Massachusetts. Second Cavalry Sgt. George Howard took his discharge at Fort Sanders, Wyoming, on May 31, 1877, and returned to his hometown of Hinsdale, New Hampshire. Here he married and started a family, but was murdered in 1887. Private James Frew of the 5th Cavalry received his discharge at Sidney Barracks, Nebraska, in January 1877. He eventually settled in Harrison, Arkansas, where he operated Frew Saddlery, one of the largest firms of its type in the Ozark Mountain country.[182]

We know of some of these veterans because their names surfaced from time to time in local newspapers, when eager reporters sought a trooper's or a doughboy's reaction to a battle anniversary or a prominent soldier's or scout's death. Even the slightest insight or anecdote from a veteran of the Little Big Horn campaign, or from one who had actually witnessed Cody's "first scalp for Custer," had appeal and legitimacy in the nation as the years rolled on and the realities of the Indian wars faded from memory. We know of a few other Great Sioux War veterans because of scattered diaries and letters bequeathed to succeeding generations. These interesting and sometimes striking documents are touchstones from a faded past that measurably upgrade our understanding of soldiering in the mid–1870s, when the Regulars "trailed the Sioux and heard the war whoop and saw the signal fires."[183]

1. For a richly rewarding, detailed study of the post–Civil War Indian-fighting army, drawn heavily from enlisted men's reminiscences, see Don Rickey, Jr., *Forty Miles a Day on Beans and Hay: The Enlisted Soldier Fighting the Indian Wars* (Norman: University of Oklahoma Press, 1963). For specific analyses of 1876–77 men, see Paul L. Hedren, "An Infantry Company in the Sioux Campaign, 1876," *Montana The Magazine of Western History* 33 (Winter 1983), 30–39; John M. Carroll, *A Bit of Seventh Cavalry History with All Its Warts* (Bryan, Tex.: Self-published, 1987); Kenneth Hammer, *Men with Custer: Biographies of the 7th Cavalry,* edited by Ronald H. Nichols (Hardin, Mont.: Custer Battlefield Historical and Museum Association, 1995); and Douglas C. McChristian, "Custer's Avengers," *Greasy Grass* 8 (May 1992), 2–10. For general identifications of other enlisted veterans of the 1876 campaign, see James Willert, *After Little Bighorn: 1876 Campaign Rosters* (LaMirada, Calif.: James Willert, Publisher, 1985).

2. In analyzing the fifty-odd enlisted men's diaries, letters, reminiscences, and memoirs of the Great Sioux War accounted for in the Bibliography, several cautions necessarily apply. Reminiscences produced in a time far removed from the era often beg careful analyses of the writer's motives, judgments, and details because memories fade, facts blur, and intents obfuscate. But date and detail imperativeness often become moot in social histories. In the cases of interviews, sometimes interrogators pressed their line of questioning so as to induce certain responses. That circumstance is often alleged about those stalwarts conducting Indian interviews, particularly of Sioux and Cheyenne participants in the Little Big Horn battle. Perhaps, indeed, the questioners knew precisely what they sought and Indians responded accordingly. In the case of the enlisted men's accounts, however, these cautions seem to apply only marginally. The stench of a battlefield, the sorrow of burying a bunky or acquaintance, or the trauma of being shot at for the very first time are irreproachable memories, whether penned under the shelter of a cottonwood tree in the valley of the Little Big Horn River two days after the episode occurred or written forty years later in the comfort of a veteran's own home. Forgotten or confused dates and miles marched become forgivable and correctable mistakes.

3. For contextual background on the Great Sioux War, see Paul L. Hedren, ed., *The Great Sioux War: The Best from* Montana The Magazine of Western History (Helena: Montana Historical Society, 1991), 1–21, 25–52; Charles

M. Robinson III, *A Good Year to Die: The Story of the Great Sioux War* (New York: Random House, 1995), 3–36; and Robert M. Utley, *the Lance and the Shield: The Life and Times of Sitting Bull* (New York: Henry Holt and Company, 1993), 106–30. On the Black Hills, see also Watson Parker, "The Majors and the Miners: The Role of the U.S. Army in the Black Hills Gold Rush," *Journal of the West* 11 (January 1972): 99–113.

4. The story of the Powder River battle is well told by J. W. Vaughn, *The Reynolds Campaign on Powder River* (Norman: University of Oklahoma Press, 1961); and Robinson, *A Good Year to Die,* chapters 6 and 7.

5. The indispensable account of the summer war, as vital today as when first published, is Edgar I. Stewart's *Custer's Luck* (Norman: University of Oklahoma Press, 1955.) Among specific accounts of the Rosebud and Little Big Horn battles, see Robinson and Utley above, plus J. W. Vaughn, *With Crook at the Rosebud* (Harrisburg, Pa.: Stackpole Company, 1956); Neil C. Mangum, *Battle of the Rosebud: Prelude to the Little Bighorn* (El Segundo, Calif.: Upton & Sons, 1987); and Larry Sklenar, *To Hell With Honor: Custer and the Little Bighorn* (Norman: University of Oklahoma Press, 2000).

6. The army's activities in southeastern Wyoming are chronicled by Paul L. Hedren in *First Scalp for Custer: The Skirmish at Warbonnet Creek, Nebraska, July 17, 1876* (Glendale, Calif.: Arthur H. Clark Company, 1980), and *Fort Laramie in 1876: Chronicle of a Frontier Post at War* (Lincoln: University of Nebraska Press, 1988).

7. Miles's relentless winter campaigning is told by Jerome A. Greene in *Yellowstone Command: Colonel Nelson A. Miles and the Great Sioux War, 1876–1877* (Lincoln: University of Nebraska Press, 1991).

8. Jerome Greene chronicles the Slim Buttes action and Starvation March in *Slim Buttes, 1876: An Episode of the Great Sioux War* (Norman: University of Oklahoma Press, 1982).

9. On the so-called Dull Knife or Red Fork of the Powder River battle, see Robinson, *A Good Year to Die,* chapters 27–29; and Jerome Greene, *Morning Star Dawn: The Powder River Expedition and the Northern Cheyennes, 1876* (Norman: University of Oklahoma Press, 2003).

10. For the Lame Deer fight and Miles's other sorties in 1877, see Greene, *Yellowstone Command,* chapters 9 and 10.

11. The sites are enumerated, with directions provided for most, in Paul L. Hedren, *Traveler's Guide to the Great Sioux War: The Battlefields, Forts, and Related Sites of America's Greatest Indian War* (Helena: Montana Historical Society Press, 1996).

12. Horn letter. Complete citations for all accounts are given in the Bibliography.

13. White reminiscence, Marquis, ed., 57.

14. Ryan reminiscence, Graham, ed., 242. A greatly augmented and annotated version of Ryan's reminiscence appeared subsequent to the principal writing of *We Trailed the Sioux*. See Sandy Barnard, ed., *Ten Years with*

Custer: A 7th Cavalryman's Memoirs (Terre Haute, Ind.: AST Press, 2001).

15. Powers letter, Dobak, ed., 96.
16. Daly reminiscence, 16.
17. Jordan diary, Greene, ed., 196.
18. Kincaid reminiscence, 1.
19. Zimmer diary, Greene, ed., 96.
20. Mears reminiscence, 74.
21. Frew diary, Hedren, ed., 449.
22. Jordan diary, Greene, ed., 195.
23. Zimmerman reminiscence.
24. Frew diary, Hedren, ed., 452.
25. Sanford diary, Hill and Innis, eds., 12, 20.
26. Mulford reminiscence, 94; Sanford diary, Hill and Innis, eds., 22; Smith diary, Smith, ed., 47.
27. Howard diary, Reneau, ed., 66.
28. Dose letter.
29. Smith diary, Smith, ed., 46.
30. Mulford reminiscence, 83.
31. Howard diary, Reneau, ed., 63.
32. John G. Bourke diary, July 11, 1877, microfilm edition of original at the United States Military Academy, Nebraska State Historical Society, Lincoln.
33. Zimmer diary, Greene, ed., 62.
34. Mulford reminiscence, 79.
35. Ryan reminiscence, Graham, ed., 241.
36. Slaper reminiscence, Brininstool, ed., 46.
37. Taylor reminiscence, 32.
38. Ryan reminiscence, Graham, ed., 241.

39. Thompson reminiscence, Brown and Willard, eds., 149.
40. Ryan reminiscence, Graham, ed., 241.
41. Slaper reminiscence, Brininstool, ed., 48.
42. Ryan reminiscence, Graham, ed., 242.
43. Smith diary, Smith, ed., 72.
44. Slaper reminiscence, Brininstool, ed., 55.
45. Ryan reminiscence, Graham, ed., 244.
46. Ibid., 245.
47. Roy interview, Hammer, ed., 114.
48. Thompson reminiscence, Brown and Willard, eds., 177. Thompson did not identify the casualty, but he was likely Pvt. Julien Jones of Company H. See Richard G. Hardorff, *The Custer Battle Casualties: Burials, Exhumations, and Reinterments* (El Segundo, Calif.: Upton and Sons, Publishers, 1989), 164.
49. O'Neill interview, Hammer, ed., 109.
50. Roy interview, Hammer, ed., 114.
51. Taylor reminiscence, 59.
52. Roy interview, Hammer, ed., 115.
53. Coleman diary, Liddic, ed., 19.
54. Slaper reminiscence, Brininstool, ed., 59; Goldin reminiscence, Brininstool, ed., 230; White reminiscence, Marquis, ed., 77. Although not an enlisted man, another memorable and timeless utterance from the Great Sioux War is attributed to Capt. Guy V. Henry of the 3rd Cavalry. Henry received a horrible facial wound in the battle of the Rosebud when a bullet passed through both cheekbones, broke the bridge of his nose, and destroyed the optic nerve of his left eye. As he lay bloodied in the

fierce summer sun, and with the battle raging about him, he dismissed condolences from newspaperman John Finerty with the remark: "It is nothing. For this we are soldiers." John Finerty, *War-Path and Bivouac; or, The Conquest of the Sioux* (Chicago: Donohue & Henneberry, 1890), 129–30.

55. Berry reminiscence, Brininstool, ed., 299.
56. White reminiscence, Marquis, ed., 68.
57. Coon reminiscence.
58. Goldin reminiscence.
59. Ibid.
60. Kanipe reminiscence, 282.
61. Goldin reminiscence.
62. White reminiscence, Marquis, ed., 82.
63. Glenn interview, Hammer, ed., 136–37.
64. Slaper reminiscence, Brininstool, ed., 61.
65. Gerard interview, Hammer, ed., 236–37.
66. Gaffney interview, Hammer, ed., 93.
67. Roy interview, Hammer, ed., 116.
68. Kennedy interview, Liddic and Harbaugh, eds., 159.
69. Thompson reminiscence, Brown and Willard, eds., 204.
70. Herendeen interview, Hammer, ed., 226.
71. Hammon interview, Hardorff, ed., 74.
72. Slaper reminiscence, Brininstool, ed., 65.
73. Carroll diary, 235; Coleman diary, Liddic, ed., 23.
74. Berry reminiscence, Brininstool, ed., 302–3.
75. Coleman diary, Liddic, ed., 24.
76. Stumpf diary.
77. Taylor reminiscence, 116.

78. Weihe (aka Charles White) diary.
79. James T. King, "General Crook at Camp Cloud Peak: 'I Am at a Loss What to Do,'" *Journal of the West* 11 (January 1972), 114–27.
80. Paul L. Hedren, "'three cool, determined men': The Sioux War Heroism of Privates Evans, Stewart, and Bell," *Montana The Magazine of Western History* 41 (Winter 1991), 14–27.
81. Howard diary, Reneau, ed., 66.
82. Hedren, "three cool, determined men," 23; Evans reminiscence, Rodenbough, ed., 321.
83. Madsen reminiscence.
84. Powers letter, Dobak, ed., 101.
85. Zimmerman reminiscence.
86. Jordan diary, Greene, ed., 195.
87. Ibid.
88. Mulford reminiscence, 70.
89. Frew diary, Hedren, ed., 140.
90. Howard diary, Reneau, ed., 72.
91. Zimmer diary, Greene, ed., 103.
92. Ibid., 71.
93. Coleman diary, Liddic, ed., 14; Thompson reminiscence, Brown and Willard, eds., 150; Edgar I. Stewart and Jane R. Stewart, eds., *The Field Diary of Lt. Edward Settle Godfrey* (Portland, Ore.: Champoeg Press, 1957), 9.
94. Roy interview, Hammer, ed., 111, referring to 1st Lt. Donald McIntosh, commanding the company.
95. White reminiscence, Marquis, ed., 74, 89.
96. Thompson reminiscence, Brown and Willard, eds., 204.

97. Smith diary, Smith, ed., 77.

98. Mulford reminiscence, 106.

99. Zimmerman reminiscence; Zimmer diary, Greene, ed., 37; Cox reminiscence, 121; Mulford reminiscence, 97; Jordan diary, Greene, ed., 194.

100. Jordan diary, Greene, ed., 194.

101. Ibid.

102. Frew diary, Hedren, ed., 145.

103. Zimmer diary, Greene, ed., 80.

104. McClellan diary, Buecker, ed., 32.

105. Mulford reminiscence, 96; Howard diary, Reneau, ed., 75; Zimmer diary, Greene, ed., 101.

106. Howard diary, Reneau, ed., 65; Cox reminiscence, 118.

107. Mulford reminiscence, 93.

108. Howard diary, Reneau, ed., 71.

109. Mulford reminiscence, 98.

110. Coleman diary, Liddic, ed., 24.

111. Ben Innis, "Bottoms Up! The Smith and Leighton Yellowstone Store Ledger of 1876," *North Dakota History* 51 (Summer 1984), 24–38.

112. Mulford reminiscence, 97.

113. Sanford diary, Hill and Innis, eds., 20.

114. Zimmer diary, Greene, ed., 21; Jordan diary, Greene, ed., 196. Regarding the song, "The Regular Army O," see Rickey, *Forty Miles a Day on Beans and Hay,* 189–90, and the original song sheet of the same name reproduced by Rickey in 1962.

115. Zimmer diary, Greene, ed., 21, 39; Meddaugh diary.

116. Jordan diary, Greene, ed., 195.

117. Sanford diary, Hill and Innis, eds., 17.
118. Howard diary, Reneau, ed., 63.
119. McClellan diary, Buecker, ed., 32.
120. *Cheyenne Daily Leader,* August 12, 1876. See the Howard, Smith, and Taylor diaries for other examples of field poetry.
121. Coleman diary, Liddic, ed., 25.
122. Meddaugh diary.
123. Smith diary, Smith, ed., 97, 99.
124. Ibid., 123.
125. Ibid., 36–37.
126. Zimmer diary, Greene, ed., 16.
127. Jordan diary, Greene, ed., 195.
128. Meddaugh diary.
129. Howard diary, Reneau, ed., 72.
130. Zimmerman reminiscence.
131. McMachin letter, Dobak, ed., 103.
132. Howard diary, Reneau, ed., 75.
133. Zimmerman reminiscence; Frew diary, Hedren, ed., 143.
134. Pollock (aka John E. Douglass) reminiscence.
135. Zimmerman reminiscence.
136. McMachin letter, Dobak, ed., 104.
137. Mears reminiscence, 73.
138. Lloyd letter.
139. Howard diary, Reneau, ed., 77.
140. Flynn diary.
141. Ibid.
142. Howard diary, Reneau, ed., 79.

143. Quoted in Jerome A. Greene, *Slim Buttes, 1876: An Episode of the Great Sioux War* (Norman: University of Oklahoma Press, 1982), note 56, 167.
144. Zimmerman reminiscence.
145. Smith diary, Smith, ed., 102.
146. Pollock reminiscence.
147. Frew letter and diary, Hedren, ed., 144, 147.
148. Zimmerman reminiscence.
149. Coleman diary, Liddic, ed., 13.
150. Zimmerman reminiscence.
151. Frew diary, Hedren, ed., 143.
152. McMachin letter, Dobak, ed., 105.
153. Jordan diary, Greene, ed., 196.
154. Zimmerman reminiscence.
155. McMachin letter, Dobak, ed., 103.
156. Frew letter, Hedren, ed., 147.
157. Ibid.
158. Flynn diary.
159. Flynn diary. See also Paul L. Hedren, "Dakota Images," *South Dakota History* 23 (Spring 1993), 100–101, reporting on the ignoble death of Pvt. John Pommer, Company I, 5th Cavalry, of dysentery.
160. Frew diary, Hedren, ed., 145.
161. Brown letter, Dobak, ed., 97.
162. Crook's command recuperated in the Black Hills for nearly one month, and photographer Stanley J. Morrow sought out members on several occasions to produce a remarkable series of photographs documenting the hag-

gard condition of the soldiers, the bleakness of their camps, and the humility of shooting and butchering horses. See Paul L. Hedren, *With Crook in the Black Hills: Stanley J. Morrow's 1876 Photographic Legacy* (Boulder, Colo.: Pruett Publishing Company, 1985).

163. Pollock reminiscence.

164. White reminiscence, Marquis, ed., 77.

165. Ibid., 97.

166. Daly reminiscence, 17.

167. John S. Collins, *My Experiences in the West* (Chicago: R. R. Donnelley & Sons Company, 1970), 158.

168. Mulford reminiscence, 26.

169. Howard diary, Reneau, ed., 62.

170. McMachin letter, Dobak, ed., 105.

171. Thompson reminiscence, Brown and Willard, eds., 207.

172. Mulford reminiscence, 111.

173. Thompson reminiscence, Brown and Willard, eds., 193–94.

174. Taylor reminiscence, 57.

175. "Regular" letter, Greene, ed., 147.

176. McBlain reminiscence, Greene, ed., 205.

177. See Charles King, *Campaigning with Crook and Stories of Army Life* (New York: Harper & Brothers, 1890), 39, 41, referencing the 5th Cavalry's arrival at Red Cloud Agency immediately following the Warbonnet Creek skirmish; and Rickey, *Forty Miles a Day on Beans and Hay,* 229–30, referencing Pvt. Charles Lester of the 4th Infantry expressing the identical sentiment at Fort

Fetterman in 1869. Mears speaks similarly in his reminiscence, 74.

178. Flynn diary.

179. Howard diary, Reneau, ed., 83.

180. Zimmerman reminiscence.

181. Zimmer diary, Greene, ed., 103, commenting on Brisbin forecasting their eating fat horses and mules if rations ran out.

182. On Stewart, Ryan, Howard, and Frew specifically, see Hedren, "three cool, determined men," 14–27; Sandy Barnard, *Custer's First Sergeant John Ryan* (Terra Haute, Ind.: AST Press, 1996); Susan C. Reneau, *The Adventures of Moccasin Joe: The True Life Story of Sgt. George S. Howard* (Missoula, Mont.: Blue Mountain Publishing, 1994); and Paul L. Hedren, "Campaigning with the 5th Cavalry: Private James B. Frew's Diary and Letters from the Great Sioux War of 1876," *Nebraska History* 65 (Winter 1984).

183. From a handwritten note on the front fly of a well-read copy of *Campaigning with Crook* by Charles King, reading in full: "Sterling Presented as a loving remembrance of the days when we trailed the Sioux and heard the war whoop and saw the signal fires. Your loving brother Cannon Oct 31st 1919."

BIBLIOGRAPHY

THE FOLLOWING IS AN ESSENTIAL COMPENDIUM OF ENLISTED soldier diaries, letters, and reminiscences from the Great Sioux War, 1876–77.

Berry, George C. (Musician, Company E, 7th Infantry, Montana Column), reminiscence in Brininstool, E. A., ed., *Troopers with Custer: Historic Incidents of the Battle of the Little Big Horn.* Harrisburg, Pa.: Stackpole Company, 1952.

Brown, Alexander (Sergeant, Company G, 7th Cavalry, Dakota Column), diary in Koury, Michael J., ed., *Diaries of the Little Big Horn.* Bellevue, Neb.: Old Army Press, 1968.

Brown, Daniel (Private, Company G, 5th Cavalry, Big Horn and Yellowstone Expedition), letter in Dobak, William A., "Yellow-Leg Journalists: Enlisted Men as Newspaper Reporters in the Sioux Campaign, 1876," *Journal of the West* 13 (January 1974).

Carroll, Matthew (Civilian Teamster, Montana Column), diary in *Contributions to the Historical Society of Montana.* Boston: J. S. Tanner and Company, 1966.

Coleman, Thomas W. (Private, Company B, 7th Cavalry, Dakota Column), diary, Liddic, Bruce R., ed., *I Buried Custer: The Diary of Pvt. Thomas W. Coleman, 7th U.S. Cavalry.* College Station, Tex.: Creative Publishing Company, 1979.

Coon, Homer L. (Private, Company G, 7th Infantry, Montana Column), reminiscence, Western Americana Collection, Coe Library, Yale University, New Haven, Conn., copy in the White Swan Library, Little Bighorn Battlefield National Monument, Crow Agency, Mont.

Cox, John E. (Sergeant, Company K, 1st Infantry, Yellowstone River Guard), reminiscence, *Five Years in the United States Army.* New York: Sol Lewis, 1973.

Daly, Henry W. (Civilian Packer, Big Horn and Yellowstone Expedition), reminiscence, "The War Path," *American Legion Monthly,* April 1927.

Dose, Henry C. (Trumpeter, Company G, 7th Cavalry, Dakota Column), letter, White Swan Library, Little Bighorn Battlefield National Monument, Crow Agency, Mont.

Evans, William (Private, Company E, 7th Infantry, Montana Column), reminiscence in Rodenbough, Theo. F., ed., *Sabre and Bayonet: Stories of Heroism and Military Adventure.* New York: G.W. Dillingham Co., 1897.

Flynn, Richard (Private, Company D, 4th Infantry, Big Horn and Yellowstone Expedition), transcribed diary, Fort Laramie National Historic Site, Fort Laramie, Wyo.

Fox, John (Private, Company D, 7th Cavalry, Dakota Column), interview in Liddic, Bruce R., and Paul Harbaugh,

Camp on Custer: Transcribing the Custer Myth. Spokane, Wash.: Arthur H. Clark Company, 1995.

Frew, James Barcus (Private, Company D, 5th Cavalry, Warbonnet Episode, Big Horn and Yellowstone Expedition), diary and letters in Hedren, Paul L., ed., "Campaigning with the 5th Cavalry: Private James B. Frew's Diary and Letters from the Great Sioux War of 1876," *Nebraska History* 65 (Winter 1984).

Gaffney, George (Sergeant, Company I, 7th Cavalry, Dakota Column), interview in Liddic, Bruce R., and Paul Harbaugh, *Camp on Custer: Transcribing the Custer Myth.* Spokane: Arthur H. Clark Company, 1995.

Gerard, Frederic Francis (Civilian Interpreter, Dakota Column), interviews in Hammer, Kenneth, ed., *Custer in '76: Walter Camp's Notes on the Custer Fight.* Provo, Utah: Brigham Young University Press, 1976.

Glenn, George W. (Private, Company H, 7th Cavalry, Dakota Column), interview in Hammer, Kenneth, ed., *Custer in '76: Walter Camp's Notes on the Custer Fight.* Provo, Utah: Brigham Young University Press, 1976.

Goldin, Theodore W. (Private, Company G, 7th Cavalry, Dakota Column), reminiscence, "Terry and Crook," *Ours, A Military Magazine,* March, May, 1888.

Hammon, John E. (Sergeant, Company G, 7th Cavalry, Dakota Column), interview in Hardorff, Richard G., ed., *Camp, Custer, and the Little Bighorn.* El Segundo, Calif.: Upton and Sons, Publishers, 1997.

Herendeen, George (Civilian Scout, Montana Column), interview in Hammer, Kenneth, ed., *Custer in '76: Walter*

Camp's Notes on the Custer Fight. Provo, Utah: Brigham Young University Press, 1976.

Horn, Marion E. (Private, Company I, 7th Cavalry, Dakota Column), letter, White Swan Library, Little Bighorn Battlefield National Monument, Crow Agency, Mont.

Howard, George Shepard (Sergeant, Company E, 2nd Cavalry, Big Horn and Yellowstone Expedition), diary in Reneau, Susan C., ed., *The Adventures of Moccasin Joe: The True Life Story of Sgt. George S. Howard*. Missoula, Mont.: Blue Mountain Publishing, 1994.

Jordan, William Walter (Private, Company C, 14th Infantry, Big Horn and Yellowstone Expedition), diary in Greene, Jerome A., ed., "Chasing Sitting Bull and Crazy Horse: Two Fourteenth U.S. Infantry Diaries of the Great Sioux War," *Nebraska History* 78 (Winter 1997).

Kanipe, Daniel Alexander (Sergeant, Company C, 7th Cavalry, Dakota Column), reminiscence, "A New Story of Custer's Last Battle," *Contributions to the Historical Society of Montana,* vol. 12. Boston: J. S. Canner and Company, 1966.

Kennedy, Francis Johnson, aka Francis Johnson (Private, Company I, 7th Cavalry, Dakota Column), interview in Liddic, Bruce R., and Paul Harbaugh, *Camp on Custer: Transcribing the Custer Myth*. Spokane: Arthur H. Clark Company, 1995.

Kincaid, James B. (Sergeant, Company B, 4th Cavalry, Powder River Expedition), reminiscence in *Winners of the West,* July 1939.

Lloyd, Thomas (Private, Company E, 3rd Cavalry, Big Horn and Yellowstone Expedition), letter, Minnesota Historical Society, St. Paul, Minn.

Lynch, Dennis (Private, Company F, 7th Cavalry, Dakota Column), interview in Hammer, Kenneth, ed., *Custer in '76: Walter Camp's Notes on the Custer Fight.* Provo, Utah: Brigham Young University Press, 1976.

Madsen, Christian (Private, Company A, 5th Cavalry, Warbonnet Episode, Big Horn and Yellowstone Expedition), reminiscence, "Five Years on the Prairies of West-America." Translated from Danish by Kirsten Fearn. Buffalo Bill Historical Center, Cody, Wyo.

Martin, John (Trumpeter, Company H, 7th Cavalry, Dakota Column), interviews in Hammer, Kenneth, ed., *Custer in '76: Walter Camp's Notes on the Custer Fight.* Provo, Utah: Brigham Young University Press, 1976.

McBlain, John F. (Private, Company L, 2nd Cavalry, Yellowstone Command), reminiscence in Greene, Jerome A., ed., *Battles and Skirmishes of the Great Sioux War, 1876–1877: The Military View.* Norman: University of Oklahoma Press, 1993.

McClellan, James S. (First Sergeant, Company H, 3rd Cavalry, Powder River Expedition), diary in Buecker, Thomas B., ed., "The Journals of James S. McClellan, 1st Sgt., Company H, 3rd Cavalry," *Annals of Wyoming* 57 (Spring 1985).

McMachin, Alfred (Private, Company E, 5th Cavalry, Big Horn and Yellowstone Expedition), letters in Dobak, William A., "Yellow-Leg Journalists: Enlisted Men as

Newspaper Reporters in the Sioux Campaign, 1876,"
Journal of the West 13 (January 1974).

Mears, David T. (Civilian Packer, Big Horn Expedition, Big
Horn and Yellowstone Expedition, Powder River Expedition), reminiscence, "Campaigning against Crazy Horse,"
in *Nebraska Proceedings and Collections.* Lincoln: Nebraska
State Historical Society, 1904.

Mechlin, Henry W. B. (Private, Company H, 7th Cavalry,
Dakota Column), interview in Hardorff, Richard G., ed.,
Camp, Custer, and the Little Bighorn. El Segundo, Calif.:
Upton and Sons, Publishers, 1997.

Meddaugh, Samuel L. (Corporal, Company I, 6th Infantry,
Yellowstone River Guard), diary, Newberry Library,
Chicago.

Mulford, Ami Frank (Trumpeter, Company M, 7th Cavalry,
Little Missouri Expedition), reminiscence, *Fighting Indians
in the 7th United States Cavalry.* Corning, N.Y.: Paul Linds-
ley Mulford, n.d.

O'Neill, Thomas F. (Private, Company G, 7th Cavalry, Dakota
Column), interview in Hammer, Kenneth, ed., *Custer in
'76: Walter Camp's Notes on the Custer Fight.* Provo, Utah:
Brigham Young University Press, 1976.

Pollock, O. C., aka John E. Douglass (Private, Company M,
3rd Cavalry, Big Horn Expedition, Big Horn and Yellowstone Expedition), reminiscence, "Veteran Recalls Hardships of Indian Fighting in West," *National Tribune,*
October 3, 1940.

Powers, John (Sergeant, Company A, 5th Cavalry, Big Horn
and Yellowstone Expedition), letters in Dobak, William A.,

"Yellow-Leg Journalists: Enlisted Men as Newspaper Reporters in the Sioux Campaign, 1876," *Journal of the West* 13 (January 1974).

"Regular" (5th Infantry, Yellowstone Command), letter in Greene, Jerome A., ed., *Battles and Skirmishes of the Great Sioux War, 1876–1877: The Military View.* Norman: University of Oklahoma Press, 1993.

Roy, Stanislas (Corporal, Company A, 7th Cavalry, Dakota Column), interview in Hammer, Kenneth, ed., *Custer in '76: Walter Camp's Notes on the Custer Fight.* Provo, Utah: Brigham Young University Press, 1976.

Ryan, John (First Sergeant, Company M, 7th Cavalry, Dakota Column), reminiscence in Graham, William A., *The Custer Myth: A Source Book of Custeriana.* New York: Bonanza Books, 1953.

Sanford, Wilmont P. (Private, Company D, 6th Infantry, Yellowstone River Guard), diary in Hill, Michael D., and Ben Innis, eds., "The Fort Buford Diary of Private Sanford, 1876–1877," *North Dakota History* 53 (Summer 1985).

Slaper, William C. (Private, Company M, 7th Cavalry, Dakota Column), reminiscence in Brininstool, E. A., ed., *Troopers with Custer: Historic Incidents of the Battle of the Little Big Horn.* Harrisburg, Pa.: Stackpole Company, 1952.

Smith, William Earl (Private, Company E, 4th Cavalry, Powder River Expedition), diary in Smith, Sherry L., ed., *Sagebrush Soldier: Private William Earl Smith's View of the Sioux War of 1876.* Norman: University of Oklahoma Press, 1989.

Stumpf, Edward R. (Private, Company A, 7th Infantry, Montana Column), diary, Henry E. Huntington Library and Art Gallery, Huntington Beach, Calif.

Taylor, William Othneil (Private, Company A, 7th Cavalry, Dakota Column), reminiscence, *With Custer on the Little Bighorn.* New York: Viking Penguin, 1996.

Thompson, Peter (Private, Company E, 7th Cavalry, Dakota Column), reminiscence in Brown, Jesse, and A. M. Willard, eds., *The Black Hills Trails.* Rapid City, S.Dak.: Rapid City Journal Company, 1924.

Weihe, Henry Charles, aka Charles White (Sergeant, Company M, 7th Cavalry, Dakota Column), diary, White Swan Library, Little Bighorn Battlefield National Monument, Crow Agency, Mont.

White, William H. (Private, Company F, 2nd Cavalry, Montana Column), reminiscence in Marquis, Thomas, *Custer, Cavalry and Crows: The Story of William White as Told to Thomas Marquis.* Fort Collins, Colo.: Old Army Press, 1975.

Zimmer, William Frederick (Private, Company F, 2nd Cavalry, Little Missouri Expedition), diary in Greene, Jerome A., ed., *Frontier Soldier: An Enlisted Man's Journal of the Sioux and Nez Perce Campaigns, 1877.* Helena: Montana Historical Society Press, 1998.

Zimmerman, John K. (Corporal, Company I, 14th Infantry, Big Horn and Yellowstone Expedition), reminiscence, Wyoming State Archives, Cheyenne, Wyo.

ABOUT THE AUTHOR

PAUL L. HEDREN'S LIFELONG INTEREST IN BLACK HILLS GOLD, Custer, and the Great Sioux War is widely known. An award-winning researcher and writer, he is the author or editor of six books and dozens of articles and introductions, mostly focusing on the Regular army and its campaigns on the northern plains. Hedren is now completing an expansive history of the dramatic afterlife enveloping Sioux Country when the Indian fighting of the 1870s ended, a story of railroads, buffalo, cattle, Indian despair, army redeployment, and memorialization. Hedren resides in O'Neill, Nebraska, where he is the National Park Service's superintendent of the Niobrara National Scenic River and Missouri National Recreational River, two units of America's Wild and Scenic Rivers System.

INDEX

Note: Page references in *italic* type indicate illustrations. The denotation "*pl.*"
followed by a number indicates a plate in the series following page 34.